Forms of Government
of North Carolina
Cities

2002

Compiled by
David M. Lawrence

INSTITUTE *of* GOVERNMENT
The University of North Carolina at Chapel Hill

Preface

While there are general law provisions for the forms of government of North Carolina cities, nearly every city operates under a charter granted by special act of the General Assembly. Since enactment of the "Home Rule Act" in 1969, these charters may be amended by local action. This publication sets out the form of government and method of election of each incorporated city, town, and village in North Carolina at the end of 2001. It was compiled from city charters and local acts amendatory thereof for each city. In addition, changes made under the "Home Rule Act" were searched at the Legislative Library, where the Act requires such changes to be filed. This information was then verified by sending proof pages to each city, town, and village listed and asking for corrections. In this manner, additional Home Rule changes were found. This publication is revised periodically, most recently in 1998.

The following terms are used:

AL	Elected at large
C–Man	Council–Manager
D	Elected by and from districts
DAL	Elected at large but candidates must meet district residence requirements
4S	4-year staggered terms
GS	General Statutes
Majority	Election decided by majority of the votes cast, with provision for runoff
May.-C	Mayor–Council
Partisan	Partisan elections
PL	Public–Local Acts (before 1943)
Plurality	Election determined by plurality
Pr	Private Acts (before 1943)
Primary	Nonpartisan primary to narrow the field to two candidates for each position to be filled; election determined by plurality
SL	Session Laws (1943 and after)

David M. Lawrence
Institute of Government
January 2002

FORMS OF GOVERNMENT AND METHODS OF ELECTION
IN NORTH CAROLINA CITIES

City (Style) [Population]	Form of Government	Governing Body	Mayor: Selection and Term	Board: Selection and Term		Election Method	Statutory Citations
ABOVE 25,000							
Asheville (City) [68,889]	C-Man.	6 Council Members & Mayor	Elected-4	AL	4S	Primary	Pr. 1931, c. 121 Pr. 1935, c. 30 SL 1969, c. 165 GS 160A-101
Burlington (City) [44,917]	C-Man.	4 Council Members & Mayor	Elected-2	AL	4S	Primary	SL 1961, c. 119 GS 160A-101
Cary (Town) [94,536]	C-Man.	6 Council Members & Mayor	Elected-4	4D 2AL	4S	Majority	SL 1971, c. 868 GS 160A-101
Chapel Hill (Town) [48,715]	C-Man.	8 Council Members & Mayor	Elected-2	AL	4S	Plurality	SL 1975, c. 473 SL 1981, c. 911 GS 160A-101
Charlotte (City) [540,828]	C-Man.	11 Council Members & Mayor	Elected-2	7D 4AL	2	Partisan	SL 2000-26
Concord (City) [55,977]	C-Man.	7 Council Members & Mayor	Elected-4	6DAL 1AL	4	Plurality	SL 1985(86), c. 861 GS 160A-101
Durham (City) [187,035]	C-Man.	6 Council Members & Mayor	Elected-2	3DAL 3AL	4S	Primary	SL 1975, c. 671 GS 160A-101
Fayetteville (City) [121,015]	C-Man.	9 Council Members & Mayor	Elected-2	D	2	Primary	SL 1979, c. 557, 794 GS 160A-101
Gastonia (City) [66,277]	C-Man.	6 Council Members & Mayor	Elected-2	DAL	2	Plurality	SL 1991, c. 557 SL 1993, c. 136
Goldsboro (City) [39,043]	C-Man.	6 Council Members & Mayor	Elected-4	D	4	Primary	SL 1973, c. 69 SL 1975, c. 245 SL 1985(86), c. 888 GS 160A-101
Greensboro (City) [223,891]	C-Man.	8 Council Members & Mayor	Elected-2	5D 3AL	2	Primary	SL 1959, c. 1137 SL 1973, c. 213 GS 160A-101

City (Style) [Population]	Form of Government	Governing Body	Mayor: Selection and Term	Board: Selection and Term		Election Method	Statutory Citations

ABOVE 25,000 (continued)

City (Style) [Population]	Form of Government	Governing Body	Mayor: Selection and Term	Board: Selection and Term		Election Method	Statutory Citations
Greenville (City) [60,476]	C-Man.	6 Council Members & Mayor	Elected-2	5D 1AL	2	Plurality	SL 1981, c. 272 GS 160A-101
Hickory (City) [37,222]	C-Man.	6 Aldermen & Mayor	Elected-4	DAL	4S	Primary	SL 1961, c. 323 SL 1967, c. 404
High Point (City) [85,839]	C-Man.	8 Council Members & Mayor	Elected-2	6D 2AL	2	Primary	SL 1979, c. 501 SL 1991, c. 40 GS 160A-101
Jacksonville (City) [66,715]	C-Man.	6 Council Members & Mayor	Elected-2	4D 2AL	2	Plurality	SL 1967, c. 911 GS 163-290 GS 160A-101
Kannapolis (City) [36,910]	C-Man.	6 Council Members & Mayor	Elected-4	AL	4S	Plurality	SL 1983, c. 191 GS 160A-101
Monroe (City) [26,228]	C-Man.	6 Council Members & Mayor	Elected-2	AL	4S	Majority	SL 2000-35
Raleigh (City) [276,093]	C-Man.	7 Council Members & Mayor	Elected-2	5D 2AL	2	Majority	SL 1949, c. 1184 SL 1957, c. 121 SL 1973, c. 319 GS 160A-101
Rocky Mount (City) [55,893]	C-Man.	7 Council Members & Mayor	Elected-4	D	4S	Majority	SL 1963, c. 938 GS 160A-101
Salisbury (City) [26,462]	C-Man.	5 Council Members	By & from Council-2	AL	2	Plurality	SL 1987, c. 205
Wilmington (City) [75,838]	C-Man.	6 Council Members & Mayor	Elected-2	AL	4S	Majority	SL 1977, c. 495
Wilson (City) [44,405]	C-Man.	7 Council Members & Mayor	Elected-2	D	2	Plurality	SL 1969, c. 136 SL 1979, c. 334 GS 160A-101
Winston-Salem (City) [185,776]	C-Man.	8 Aldermen & Mayor	Elected-4	D	4	Partisan	Pr. 1927, c. 232 Pr. 1933, c. 60 SL 1947, c. 601 SL 1965, c. 53 GS 163-279

City (Style) [Population]	Form of Government	Governing Body	Mayor: Selection and Term	Board: Selection and Term		Election Method	Statutory Citations
10,000 to 25,000							
Albemarle (Town) [15,680]	C-Man.	7 Council Members & Mayor	Elected-2	4D 3AL	4S	Partisan	SL 1979, c. 259 SL 1987(88), c. 881 GS 160A-101
Apex (Town) [20,212]	C-Man.	5 Commissioners & Mayor	Elected-2	AL	4S	Plurality	SL 1985, c. 356
Asheboro (Town) [21,672]	C-Man.	7 Council Members & Mayor	Elected-4	AL	4S	Primary	SL 1967, c. 481 SL 1989(90), c. 921 GS 160A-101
Boone (Town) [13,472]	C-Man.	5 Council Members & Mayor	Elected-2	AL	4/2S[1]	Majority	Pr. 1907, c. 107 Pr. 1931, c. 187 SL 1969, c. 905 GS 160A-101
Carrboro (Town) [16,782]	C-Man.	6 Aldermen & Mayor	Elected-2	AL	4S	Plurality	SL 1987, c. 476
Clemmons (Village) [13,827]	C-Man.	4 Council Members & Mayor	Elected-2	AL	4S	Plurality	SL 1985, c. 437
Cornelius (Town) [11,969]	C-Man.	5 Commissioners & Mayor	Elected-2	AL	2	Plurality	SL 1971, c. 288 SL 1991(92), c. 852
Eden (City) [15,908]	C-Man.	7 Council Members & Mayor	Elected-4	DAL	4S	Plurality	SL 1967, c. 967 SL 1969, c. 781 GS 160A-101 GS 163-290
Elizabeth City (City) [17,188]	C-Man.	8 Council Members & Mayor	Elected-2	D	2	Majority	SL 2001-227
Garner (Town) [17,757]	C-Man.	5 Aldermen & Mayor	Elected-2	AL	4S	Plurality	SL 1977, c. 333 GS 160A-101
Graham (City) [12,833]	C-Man	5 Council Members	By & from Council-2	AL	4/2S[1]	Plurality	SL 1979, c. 339
Havelock (Town) [22,442]	C-Man.	5 Commissioners & Mayor	Elected-4	AL	4S	Plurality	SL 1959, c. 952 SL 1977, c. 152 SL 1995(96), c. 619 SL 1999-126 GS 160A-66

10,000 to 25,000 (continued)

City (Style) [Population]	Form of Government	Governing Body	Mayor: Selection and Term	Board: Selection and Term		Election Method	Statutory Citations
Henderson (City) [16,095]	C-Man.	8 Council Members & Mayor	Elected-2	4D 4AL	2	Majority	SL 1967, c. 780 SL 1997-62 GS 160A-101
Hendersonville (City) [10,420]	C-Man.	4 Council Members & Mayor	Elected-4	AL	4S	Primary	SL 1971, c. 874 GS 160A-101
Hope Mills (Town) [11,237]	C-Man.	5 Commissioners & Mayor	Elected-2	AL	2	Plurality	SL 1981, c. 650
Huntersville (Town) [24,960]	C-Man.	5 Commissioners & Mayor	Elected-2	AL	2	Plurality	Pr. 1885, c. 46 GS 160A-66 GS 160A-101
Indian Trail (Town) [11,905]	May.-C	5 Council Members & Mayor	Elected-4	AL	4S	Plurality	SL 1969, c. 825
Kernersville (Town) [17,126]	C-Man.	5 Aldermen & Mayor	Elected-2	AL	2	Plurality	SL 1989, c. 381 GS 160A-101
Kinston (City) [23,688]	C-Man.	5 Council Members & Mayor	Elected-4	AL	4S	Partisan	SL 1987, c. 169
Laurinburg (City) [15,874]	C-Man.	5 Council Members & Mayor	Elected-4	4D 1AL	4S	Plurality	SL 1989, c. 586 SL 1995, c. 65 GS 160A-101
Lenoir (City) [16,793]	C-Man.	7 Council Members & Mayor	Elected-4	AL	4S	Primary	SL 1977, c. 118 SL 1997-262
Lexington (City) [19,953]	C-Man.	8 Council Members & Mayor	Elected-2	6D 2AL	4S	Plurality	SL 1981, c. 906 SL 1987, c. 64
Lumberton (City) [20,795]	C-Man.	8 Council Members & Mayor	Elected-4	D	4S	Plurality	SL 1963, c. 115 SL 1965, c. 282 SL 1967, c. 237 SL 1971, c. 166 GS 163-290
Matthews (Town) [22,127]	C-Man.	6 Commissioners & Mayor	Elected-2	AL	2	Plurality	Pr. 1879, c. 60 Pr. 1911, c. 172 SL 1951, c. 179 GS 160A-101
Mint Hill (Town) [14,922]	May.-C[2]	4 Commissioners & Mayor	Elected-2	AL	2	Plurality	SL 1971, c. 73 GS 160A-101

City (Style) [Population]	Form of Government	Governing Body	Mayor: Selection and Term	Board: Selection and Term		Election Method	Statutory Citations
10,000 to 25,000 (continued)							
Mooresville (Town) [18,823]	C-Man.	6 Commissioners & Mayor	Elected-2	4D 2AL	4S	Primary	SL 1975, c. 239 GS 160A-101
Morganton (City) [17,310]	C-Man.	4 Council Members & Mayor	Elected-4	DAL	4S	Majority	SL 1975, c. 180 SL 1998-81
New Bern (City) [23,128]	C-Man.	6 Aldermen & Mayor	Elected-4	D	4	Majority	SL 1957, c. 1281 SL 1983, c. 174 SL 1985, c. 64 GS 160A-101
Newton (City) [12,560]	C-Man.	6 Aldermen & Mayor	Elected-2	AL	4S	Plurality	SL 1989(90), c. 1042
Reidsville (City) [14,485]	C-Man.	6 Council Members & Mayor	Elected-4	4D 2AL	4S	Plurality[3]	SL 1989(90), c. 957 SL 1993, c. 306
Roanoke Rapids (City) [16,957]	C-Man.	5 Council Members & Mayor	Elected-4	D	4S	Plurality	SL 1995, c. 34
Sanford (City) [23,220]	C-Man.	7 Council Members & Mayor	Elected-4	5D 2AL	4S	Plurality	SL 1967, c. 650 SL 1997-245 GS 163-290 GS 160A-101
Shelby (City) [19,477]	C-Man.	6 Council Members & Mayor	Elected-4	DAL	4S	Majority	PL1939, c. 252 SL 1961, c. 416, 509 GS 160A-101 GS 163-290
Smithfield (Town) [11,510]	C-Man.	7 Council Members & Mayor	Elected-2	3D 4AL	4S	Plurality	Pr. 1933, c. 36, 61 SL 1959, c. 56 SL 1965, c. 827 SL 1989, c. 203
Southern Pines (Town) [10,918]	C-Man.	4 Council Members & Mayor	Elected-2	AL	2	Primary	SL 1981, c. 352 GS 160A-101
Statesville (City) [23,320]	C-Man.	8 Council Members & Mayor	Elected-4	6D 2AL	4S	Majority	SL 1977, c. 289 SL 1985, c. 570 GS 160A-101
Tarboro (Town) [11,138]	C-Man.	8 Council Members & Mayor	Elected-4	D	4S	Plurality	SL 1995, c. 73

City (Style) [Population]	Form of Government	Governing Body	Mayor: Selection and Term	Board: Selection and Term		Election Method	Statutory Citations
10,000 to 25,000 (continued)							
Thomasville (City) [19,788]	C-Man.	7 Council Members & Mayor	Elected-2	5D 2AL	2/4S[4]	Plurality	SL 1981, c. 211 GS 160A-101
Wake Forest (Town) [12,558]	C-Man.	5 Commissioners & Mayor	Elected-4	AL	4S	Plurality	SL 1973, c. 273 SL 1993, c. 118

---

1. Three board members elected every 2 years. The 2 elected with highest vote serve 4 years; the 1 elected with lowest vote serves 2 years.
2. Board appoints town administrator to supervise all departments.
3. Council members are elected pursuant to the plurality method. The mayor is elected by the "majority" method, except that a candidate can win the election with 40%, rather than 50%, of the vote.
4. Council members elected at large serve 2-year terms; council members elected from districts serve 4-year terms.

City (Style) [Population]	Form of Government	Governing Body	Mayor: Selection and Term	Board: Selection and Term		Election Method	Statutory Citations
5,000 to 10,000							
Archdale (City) [9,014]	C-Man.	6 Council Members & Mayor	Elected-2	DAL	4S	Plurality	SL 1969, c. 667
Belmont (City) [8,705]	C-Man.	5 Council Members & Mayor	Elected-4	AL	4S	Plurality	Pr. 1921, c. 22 Pr. 1935, c. 161 SL 1947, c. 125 SL 1969, c. 930 GS 160A-101
Bessemer City (City) [5,119]	C-Man.	6 Council Members & Mayor	Elected-2	DAL	2	Plurality	SL 1989(90), c. 1018
Black Mountain (Town) [7,511]	C-Man.	5 Aldermen & Mayor	Elected-4	AL	4S	Plurality	SL 1951, c. 747 SL 1969, c. 1034 GS 160A-101
Brevard (City) [6,789]	C-Man.	5 Council Members & Mayor	Elected-2	AL	4S	Plurality	SL 1981, c. 415
Cherryville (City) [5,361]	C-Man.	4 Commissioners & Mayor	Elected-2	DAL	4S	Plurality	SL 1969, c. 581
Clayton (Town) [6,973]	C-Man.	5 Council Members & Mayor	Elected-4[1]	AL	4S	Plurality	SL 1987(88), c. 983 GS 160A-101
Clinton (Town) [8,600]	C-Man.	5 Council Members & Mayor	Elected-2	D	4S	Plurality	SL 1985(86), c. 943 SL 1989(90), c. 887
Conover (City) [6,604]	C-Man.	5 Council Members & Mayor	Elected-4	AL	4S	Plurality	SL 1977, c. 78 GS 160A-101
Davidson (Town) [7,139]	May.-C	5 Commissioners & Mayor	Elected-2	AL	2	Plurality	Pr. 1879, c. 32 SL 1957, c. 36 GS 163-279
Dunn (City) [9,196]	C-Man.	6 Council Members & Mayor	Elected-4	D	4	Majority	SL 1969, c. 818 SL 1971, c. 104 GS 160A-101
Edenton (Town) [5,394]	C-Man.	6 Council Members & Mayor	Elected-4	4D 2AL	4S	Plurality	SL 1985(86), c. 815
Elon College (Town) [6,738]	C-Man.	5 Aldermen & Mayor	Elected-4	AL	4S	Plurality	SL 1985, c. 109
Forest City (Town) [7,549]	C-Man.	5 Council Members & Mayor	Elected-2	AL	2	Plurality	SL 1981, c. 209

City (Style) [Population]	Form of Government	Governing Body	Mayor: Selection and Term	Board: Selection and Term		Election Method	Statutory Citations
5,000 to 10,000 (continued)							
Fuquay-Varina (Town) [7,898]	C-Man.	5 Commissioners & Mayor	Elected-2	AL	4S	Plurality	Pr. 1915, c. 167 SL 1959, c. 774
Hamlet (Town) [6,018]	May.-C[2]	5 Commissioners & Mayor	Elected-2	AL	4S	Primary	SL 1969, c. 506 GS 160A-101
Hillsborough (Town) [5,446]	C-Man.	5 Commissioners & Mayor	Elected-2	AL	4S	Plurality	SL 1985, c. 351 GS 160A-101
Holly Springs (Town) [9,192]	C-Man.	5 Commissioners & Mayor	Elected-4	AL	4	Plurality	SL 1951, c. 110 GS 160A-101
Kill Devil Hills (Town) [5,897]	C-Man.	4 Commissioners & Mayor	Elected-2	AL	4S	Plurality	SL 1995(96), c. 735
King (City) [5,952]	C-Man.	4 Council Members & Mayor	Elected-4	AL	4S	Plurality	SL 1983, c. 351 GS 160A-101
Kings Mountain (City) [9,693]	C-Man.	7 Council Members & Mayor	Elected-2	5D 2AL	2	Majority	SL 1947, c. 684 SL 1951, c. 836 SL 1969, c. 204 GS 160A-101
Knightdale (Town) [5,958]	C-Man.	5 Council Members & Mayor	Elected-4	AL	4S	Plurality	Pr. 1927, c. 155 GS 160A-101
Lewisville (Town) [8,826]	C-Man.	6 Council Members & Mayor	Elected-2	AL	2	Plurality	SL 1991, c. 116
Lincolnton (Town) [9,965]	C-Man.	4 Council Members & Mayor	Elected-2	DAL	4S	Partisan	SL 1979, c. 341 SL 1981(82), c. 1134
Mebane (City) [7,284]	C-Man.	5 Council Members & Mayor	Elected-4	AL	4S	Plurality	SL 1973, c. 514 GS 160A-101
Morehead City (Town) [7,691]	C-Man.	5 Commissioners & Mayor	Elected-2	AL	4S	Plurality	SL 1969, c. 879 GS 160A-101
Morrisville (Town) [5,208]	C-Man.[3]	5 Commissioners & Mayor	Elected-4	3DAL 2AL	4S	Plurality	SL 1947, c. 776 SL 1975, c. 802 GS 160A-101

City (Style) [Population]	Form of Government	Governing Body	Mayor: Selection and Term	Board: Selection and Term		Election Method	Statutory Citations

5,000 to 10,000 (continued)

City (Style) [Population]	Form of Government	Governing Body	Mayor: Selection and Term	Board: Selection and Term		Election Method	Statutory Citations
Mount Airy (City) [8,484]	C-Man.[3]	5 Commissioners & Mayor	Elected-4	4DAL 1AL	4S	Primary	SL 1943, c. 496 SL 1949, c. 244 SL 1995, c. 30
Mount Holly (City) [9,618]	C-Man.	6 Council Members & Mayor	Elected-2	AL	4S	Plurality	SL 1975, c. 212
Oak Island (Town) [6,571]	C-Man.	8 Council Members & Mayor	Elected-2	AL[4]	4S[4]	Plurality	SL 1999-66
Oxford (City) [8,838]	C-Man.	7 Commissioners & Mayor	Elected-2	AL	4S	Plurality	SL 1963, c. 971
Pinehurst (Village) [9,706]	C-Man.	5 Council Members	Elected[5]-4	AL	4S	Plurality	Mun. Bd. Control 1980 GS 160A-101
Rockingham (City) [9,672]	C-Man.	5 Council Members & Mayor	Elected-2	AL	2/4S[6]	Plurality	SL 1974, c. 1265 SL 1995(96), c. 698 SL 2001-68
Roxboro (City) [8,696]	C-Man.	5 Council Members & Mayor	Elected-2	AL	2	Majority	SL 1997-282
Selma (Town) [5,914]	C-Man.	4 Council Members & Mayor	Elected-2	AL	4S	Plurality	SL 1991(92), c. 934
Siler City (Town) [6,966]	C-Man.[3]	7 Commissioners & Mayor	Elected-2	5D 2AL	4S	Plurality	Pr. 1887, c. 88 SL 1989, c. 16
Spring Lake (Town) [8,098]	C-Man.	5 Aldermen & Mayor	Elected-2	AL	2	Plurality	SL 1977, c. 742 GS 160A-101
Summerfield (Town) [7,018]	May.-C	6 Council Members	2[7]	AL	2	Plurality	SL 1995, c. 426
Trinity (City) [6,690]	C-Man.	8 Council Members & Mayor	Elected-4	DAL	4S	Plurality	SL 1997-94 GS 160A-101
Washington (City) [9,583]	C-Man.	5 Council Members & Mayor	Elected-2	AL	2	Majority	SL 1995 (96), c. 736
Waynesville (Town) [9,232]	C-Man.	4 Aldermen & Mayor	Elected-4	AL	4	Majority	SL 1995, c. 126
Weddington (Town) [6,696]	May.-C	4 Council Members & Mayor	Elected-2	DAL	4S	Plurality	SL 1983, c. 256 GS 160A-101

City (Style) [Population]	Form of Government	Governing Body	Mayor: Selection and Term	Board: Selection and Term		Election Method	Statutory Citations
5,000 to 10,000 (continued)							
Whiteville (City) [5,148]	C-Man.	4 Council Members & Mayor	Elected-2	AL	4S	Plurality	SL 1987(88), c. 1018
Williamston (Town) [5,843]	May.-C[6]	5 Commissioners & Mayor	Elected-4	4D 1AL	4	Plurality	Pr. 1901, c. 129 SL 1991, c. 374 GS 160A-101

1. The 4-year term for mayor of Clayton becomes effective in 2003.
2. Council employs town administrator to supervise all departments.
3. Council–manager form established by ordinance.
4. This represents the final structure of the town council of Oak Island, which becomes fully effective in 2005. Until then, some council members are elected from residential districts representing the former towns of Long Beach and Yaupon Beach, and some terms are 2 years.
5. The direct election of the mayor of Pinehurst becomes effective in 2003.
6. Three board members elected every 2 years. The 2 elected with highest vote serve 4 years; the 1 elected with lowest vote serves 2 years.
7. The council member receiving the highest number of votes.

City (Style) [Population]	Form of Government	Governing Body	Mayor: Selection and Term	Board: Selection and Term		Election Method	Statutory Citations

2,500 to 5,000

City (Style) [Population]	Form of Government	Governing Body	Mayor: Selection and Term	Board: Selection and Term		Election Method	Statutory Citations
Aberdeen (Town) [3,400]	C-Man.	5 Commissioners & Mayor	Elected-2	AL	4S	Plurality	SL 1975, c. 147 GS 160A-101
Ahoskie (Town) [4,523]	C-Man.	5 Council Members & Mayor	Elected-2	4D 1AL	4S	Plurality	SL 1963, c. 609 GS 160A-101
Angier (Town) [3,419]	May.-C	4 Commissioners & Mayor	Elected-2	DAL	4S	Plurality	SL 1975, c. 652
Ayden (Town) [4,622]	C-Man.	5 Commissioners & Mayor	Elected-2	DAL	2	Plurality	SL 1965, c. 79 GS 163-279
Beaufort (Town) [3,771]	C-Man.	5 Commissioners & Mayor	Elected-2	AL	4S	Plurality	Pr. 1913, c. 435 Pr. 1919, c. 103 GS 160A-101
Benson (Town) [2,923]	C-Man.	6 Commissioners & Mayor	Elected-2	3D 3AL[1]	4S	Plurality	SL 1999-91 GS 160A-101
Boiling Spring Lakes (City) [2,972]	May.-C	4 Commissioners & Mayor	Elected-2	AL	4S	Plurality	SL 1977, c. 62
Boiling Springs (Town) [3,866]	May.-C	5 Commissioners & Mayor	Elected-4	AL	4S	Plurality	SL 1953, c. 349
Burgaw (Town) [3,337]	C-Man.	5 Commissioners & Mayor	Elected-4	AL	4S	Plurality	SL 2001-247
Cajah's Mountain (Town) [2,683]	May.-C	5 Aldermen	By & from Board[2]	AL	4S	Plurality	SL 1983, c. 52
Canton (Town) [4,029]	C-Man.	4 Aldermen & Mayor	Elected-2	AL	2	Plurality	Pr. 1907, c. 90 Pr. 1911, c. 178 Pr. 1935, c. 119 GS 160A-101
Carolina Beach (Town) [4,701]	C-Man.	4 Council Members & Mayor	Elected-2	AL	4S	Majority	SL 1973, c. 376 SL 1981, c. 842
China Grove (Town) [3,616]	C-Man.	5 Aldermen & Mayor	Elected-4	AL	4S	Plurality	Pr. 1903, c. 309 SL 1999-7 SL 2000-10
Cramerton (Town) [2,976]	C-Man.	5 Commissioners & Mayor	Elected-2	AL	2	Plurality	SL 1967, c. 1061 GS 160A-101
Dallas (Town) [3,402]	May.-C	5 Aldermen & Mayor	Elected-2	AL	2	Plurality	SL 1979, c. 342

11

City (Style) [Population]	Form of Government	Governing Body	Mayor: Selection and Term	Board: Selection and Term		Election Method	Statutory Citations

2,500 to 5,000 (continued)

City (Style) [Population]	Form of Government	Governing Body	Mayor: Selection and Term	Board: Selection and Term		Election Method	Statutory Citations
Elizabethtown (Town) [3,698]	C-Man.	6 Commissioners & Mayor	Elected-4	AL	4S	Plurality	Pr. 1895, c. 156 GS 160A-101
Elkin (Town) [4,109]	C-Man.	5 Commissioners & Mayor	Elected-4	AL	4S	Plurality	SL 1987, c. 740
Emerald Isle (Town) [3,488]	C-Man.	5 Commissioners & Mayor	Elected-2	AL	2	Plurality	SL 1973, c. 526 GS 160A-101
Erwin (Town) [4,537]	C-Man.	6 Commissioners & Mayor	Elected-4	AL	4	Majority	SL 1967, c. 12 GS 160A-101
Fairmont (Town) [2,604]	C-Man.	6 Commissioners & Mayor	Elected-4	AL	4S	Plurality	SL 1973, c. 288 GS 160A-101
Farmville (Town) [4,302]	C-Man.	5 Commissioners & Mayor	Elected-2	AL	4S	Majority	SL 1979, c. 406 GS 160A-101
Flat Rock (Village) [2,565]	May.-C	6 Council Members & Mayor	Elected-4	DAL	4S	Primary	SL 1995, c. 48
Fletcher (Town) [4,185]	C-Man.	4 Council Members & Mayor	Elected-4	DAL	4S	Primary	SL 1989, c. 44 GS 160A-101
Franklin (Town) [3,490]	May.-C	6 Aldermen & Mayor	Elected-2	AL	4S	Plurality	Pr. 1905, c. 26 Pr. 1935, c. 5 GS 160A-66, -101
Gamewell (Town) [3,644]	May.-C	5 Commissioners & Mayor	Elected-2	AL	4S	Plurality	SL 1981, c. 31
Gibsonville (Town) [4,372]	C-Man.	5 Aldermen & Mayor	Elected-4	AL	4S	Plurality	SL 1979, c. 392
Granite Falls (Town) [4,612]	C-Man.	6 Council Members & Mayor	Elected-4	AL	4S	Plurality	SL 1981, c. 382
Harrisburg (Town) [4,493]	May.-C	7 Council Members & Mayor	Elected-2	AL	2	Plurality	SL 1973, c. 111 GS 160A-101
Hudson (Town) [3,078]	C-Man.	6 Commissioners & Mayor	Elected-2	AL	4S	Plurality	Pr. 1905, c. 239 SL 1967, c. 322 GS 160A-101
Jamestown (Town) [3,088]	C-Man.	4 Council Members & Mayor	Elected-2	AL	2	Primary	SL 1981, c. 370

City (Style) [Population]	Form of Government	Governing Body	Mayor: Selection and Term	Board: Selection and Term		Election Method	Statutory Citations
2,500 to 5,000 (continued)							
Kitty Hawk (Town) [2,991]	C-Man.	5 Council Members	By & from Council[3]	AL	4S	Plurality	SL 1981, c. 206 GS 160A-101
LaGrange (Town) [2,844]	May.-C	6 Commissioners & Mayor	Elected-4	AL	4S	Partisan	SL 1979(80), c. 1151
Landis (Town) [2,996]	May.-C	4 Aldermen & Mayor	Elected-2	AL	2	Plurality	SL 1975, c. 213 SL 1987, c. 13 GS 160A-101
Liberty (Town) [2,661]	C-Man.	5 Council Members & Mayor	Elected-2	AL	4S	Plurality	SL 1981, c. 579
Lillington (Town) [2,915]	C-Man.	5 Commissioners & Mayor	Elected-4	AL	4S	Plurality	Pr. 1903, c. 252 SL 1959, c. 901 GS 160A-101 GS 163-290
Long View (Town) [4,722]	May.-C	5 Aldermen & Mayor	Elected-4	D	4S	Plurality	SL 1983, c. 58 GS 163-279 GS 160A-101
Louisburg (Town) [3,111]	May.-C	6 Council Members & Mayor	Elected-4	AL	4S	Plurality	SL 1961, c. 1022 GS 160A-101
Lowell (City) [2,662]	C-Man.	5 Council Members & Mayor	Elected-2	AL	2	Plurality	SL 1993, c. 111
Maiden (Town) [3,282]	C-Man.	5 Council Members & Mayor	Elected-2	AL	4/2S[4]	Plurality	Pr. 1883, c. 103 PL 1939, c. 350 SL 1955, c. 445 GS 160A-101
Marion (City) [4,943]	C-Man.	5 Council Members & Mayor	Elected-4	AL	4S	Plurality	SL 1977, c. 101
Maxton (Town) [2,551]	C-Man.	5 Commissioners & Mayor	Elected-4	AL	4S	Plurality	SL 1971, c. 731 GS 160A-101
Midland (Town) [2,567]	May.-C	4 Council Members & Mayor	Elected-4	AL	4S	Plurality	SL 2000-91
Mocksville (Town) [4,178]	C-Man.	5 Commissioners & Mayor	Elected-4	AL	4S	Plurality	SL 1963, c. 74 GS 160A-101

City (Style) [Population]	Form of Government	Governing Body	Mayor: Selection and Term	Board: Selection and Term		Election Method	Statutory Citations
2,500 to 5,000 (continued)							
Mount Olive (Town) [4,567]	C-Man.	5 Commissioners & Mayor	Elected-2	4D 1AL	2	Plurality	Pr. 1905, c. 201 SL 1977, c. 476 SL 1979(80), c. 1303 GS 160A-101
Nags Head (Town) [2,700]	C-Man.[5]	4 Commissioners & Mayor	Elected-4	AL	4S	Plurality	SL 1961, c. 808 SL 1963, c. 148 SL 1969, c. 62 GS 160A-101
Nashville (Town) [4,309]	C-Man.	4 Commissioners & Mayor	Elected-4	AL	4S	Plurality	SL 1969, c. 320 SL 1973, c. 343 GS 160A-101
Newport (Town) [3,349]	C-Man.	5 Council Members & Mayor	Elected-4	AL	4S	Plurality	Pr. 1927, c. 225 SL 1969, c. 495 GS 160A-101
North Wilkesboro (Town) [4,116]	C-Man.	5 Commissioners & Mayor	Elected-4	AL	4S	Partisan	SL 1977, c. 263
Oak Ridge (Town) [3,988]	May.-C	5 Council Members	By & from Council[3]	AL	4S	Plurality	SL 1998-113
Pineville (Town) [3,449]	May.-C	4 Council Members & Mayor	Elected-2	AL	2	Plurality	SL 1965, c. 296
Pleasant Garden (Town) [4,714]	May.-C	5 Council Members	By & from Council[3]	AL	4S	Primary	SL 1997-344
Plymouth (Town) [4,107]	C-Man.	6 Council Members & Mayor	Elected-2	D	2	Plurality	SL 1995, c. 325 SL 2001-51
Raeford (City) [3,386]	C-Man.	5 Council Members & Mayor	Elected-4	AL	4S	Plurality	SL 1973, c. 371 GS 160A-101
Randleman (City) [3,557]	C-Man.	5 Aldermen & Mayor	Elected-4	4DAL 1AL	4S 2	Plurality	Pr. 1905, c. 209 SL 1959, c. 701 GS 160A-101
Red Oak (Town) [2,723] 1035	May.-C	4 Commissioners & Mayor	Elected-4	AL	4S	Plurality	SL 1961, c. 799 SL 1989(90), c.
Red Springs (Town) [3,493]	C-Man.	6 Commissioners & Mayor	Elected-2	AL	4S	Plurality	SL 1949, c. 1252 SL 1951, c. 344 SL 1957, c. 457 SL 1969, c. 212

City (Style) [Population]	Form of Government	Governing Body	Mayor: Selection and Term	Board: Selection and Term		Election Method	Statutory Citations
River Bend (Town) [2,923]	C-Man.	5 Council Members & Mayor	Elected-2	AL	2	Plurality	Mun. Bd. Control 1981 GS 160A-66 GS 160A-101
Rutherfordton (Town) [4,131]	C-Man.	4 Council Members & Mayor	Elected-4	AL	4S	Plurality	SL 1979, c. 350 GS 160A-101
Sawmills (Town) [4,921]	May.-C	5 Council Members & Mayor	Elected-4	AL	4S	Primary	SL 1987, c. 648
Spencer (City) [3,355]	C-Man.	6 Aldermen & Mayor	Elected-2	AL	2	Plurality	Pr. 1905, c. 37 PL 1939, c. 222 SL 1951, c. 325 SL 1957, c. 870 GS 160A-101
Spindale (Town) [4,022]	C-Man.	5 Commissioners & Mayor	Elected-4	AL	4S	Plurality	SL 1975, c. 378 GS 160A-101
Stallings (Town) [3,189]	May.-C[6]	6 Council Members & Mayor	Elected-2	DAL	4S	Plurality	SL 1975, c. 758 GS 160A-101
Stanley (Town) [3,053]	C-Man.	5 Aldermen & Mayor	Elected-2	DAL	4S	Plurality	Pr. 1911, c. 233 GS 160A-101
Stokesdale (Town) [3,267]	May.-C	5 Council Members	By & from Council[3]	AL	4S	Plurality	SL 1989, c. 488
Tabor City (Town) [2,509]	C-Man.	4 Commissioners & Mayor	Elected-2	AL	4S	Plurality	Pr. 1905, c. 40 Pr. 1935, c. 18 SL 1957, c. 255 GS 160A-101
Trent Woods (Town) [4,192]	May.-C	3 Commissioners & Mayor	Elected-2	AL	2	Plurality	SL 1959, c. 718 GS 163-279
Troy (Town) [3,430]	C-Man.	5 Commissioners & Mayor	Elected-2	AL	4S	Plurality	Pr. 1883, c. 153 Pr. 1913, c. 342 SL 1957, c. 125 GS 160A-101
Unionville (Town) [4,797]	May-C	5 Commissioners & Mayor	Elected-4	AL	4S	Plurality	SL 1998-151 SL 1999-90
Valdese (Town) [4,485]	C-Man.	5 Council Members & Mayor	Elected-4	DAL	4S	Plurality	SL 1977, c. 847 SL 2000-28

City (Style) [Population]	Form of Government	Governing Body	Mayor: Selection and Term	Board: Selection and Term		Election Method	Statutory Citations

2,500 to 5,000 (continued)

City (Style) [Population]	Form of Government	Governing Body	Mayor: Selection and Term	Board: Selection and Term		Election Method	Statutory Citations
Wadesboro (Town) [3,552]	C-Man.	5 Council Members & Mayor	Elected-2	AL	4S	Plurality	SL 1975, c. 297
Walkertown (Town) [4,009]	C-Man.	4 Council Members & Mayor	Elected-2	AL	2	Plurality	SL 1983(84), c. 936 GS 160A-101
Wallace (Town) [3,344]	C-Man.	5 Council Members & Mayor	Elected-4	AL	4S	Plurality	SL 1987, c. 94 SL 1997-321
Warsaw (Town) [3,051]	May.-C	5 Commissioners & Mayor	Elected-4	AL	4S	Plurality	Pr. 1885, c. 91 SL 1965, c. 972
Waxhaw (Town) [2,625]	May.-C	5 Commissioners & Mayor	Elected-4	AL	4	Plurality	Pr. 1919, c. 57 PL 1941, c. 255 GS 160A-101
Wendell (Town) [4,247]	C-Man.	5 Commissioners & Mayor	Elected-4	AL	4S	Plurality	SL 1985, c. 107
Wentworth (Town) [2,779]	May.-C	5 Council Members	By & from Board-2	AL	4S	Plurality	SL 1997-322
Wesley Chapel (Village) [2.549]	May.-C	4 Council Members & Mayor	Elected-2	AL	4S	Plurality	SL 1998-43
Wilkesboro (Town) [3,159]	May.-C	4 Commissioners & Mayor	Elected-4	AL	4S	Plurality	Pr. 1889, c. 240 SL 1979, c. 645 GS 160A-101
Winterville (Town) [4,791]	C-Man.	5 Aldermen & Mayor	Elected-4	AL	4S	Plurality	SL 1993(94), c. 603 GS 160A-101
Woodfin (Town) [3,162]	May.-C	6 Aldermen & Mayor	Elected-2	AL	4S	Partisan	SL 1971, c. 271 SL 1979, c. 324 SL 1983, c. 291
Wrightsville Beach (Town) [2,593]	C-Man.	4 Aldermen & Mayor	Elected-2	AL	4S	Plurality	SL 1989, c. 611

City (Style) [Population]	Form of Government	Governing Body	Mayor: Selection and Term	Board: Selection and Term		Election Method	Statutory Citations
2,500 to 5,000 (continued)							
Yadkinville (Town) [2,818]	May.-C[6]	5 Commissioners & Mayor	Elected-4	AL	4S	Plurality	Pr. 1885, c. 10 SL 1979, c. 280 GS 160A-101
Zebulon (Town) [4,046]	C-Man.	5 Commissioners & Mayor	Elected-4	AL	4S	Plurality	SL 1973, c. 386 GS 160A-101

1. In the election for at-large members, each voter may only vote for 1 candidate.
2. The board elects a chairperson, who has duties of mayor. The charter does not specify if chairperson serves for a term or at the pleasure of the board.
3. Mayor serves at pleasure of Council.
4. Three board members elected every 2 years. The 2 elected with highest vote serve 4 years; the 1 elected with lowest vote serves 2 years.
5. Council–manager form established by ordinance.
6. Council employs town administrator to supervise all departments.

City (Style) [Population]	Form of Government	Governing Body	Mayor: Selection and Term	Board: Selection and Term		Election Method	Statutory Citations

1,000 to 2,500

City (Style) [Population]	Form of Government	Governing Body	Mayor: Selection and Term	Board: Selection and Term		Election Method	Statutory Citations
Andrews (Town) [1,602]	May.-C	4 Aldermen & Mayor	Elected-4	AL	4	Plurality	Pr. 1905, c. 135 Pr. 1930, c. 187 SL 1959, c. 193 SL 1977, c. 209 GS 160A-101
Atlantic Beach (Town) [1,781]	May.-C	5 Commissioners & Mayor	Elected-4	AL	4S	Plurality	PL 1937, c. 433 GS 160A-101
Badin (Town) [1,154]	C-Man.	5 Council Members	By & from Board-2	2DAL 3AL	4S	Plurality	SL 1989(90), c. 894
Belhaven (Town) [1,968]	C-Man.	5 Aldermen & Mayor	Elected-2	DAL	4S	Plurality	SL 1969, c. 714
Bermuda Run (Town) [1,431]	C-Man.	5 Council Members & Mayor	Elected-4	D	4S	Primary	SL 1999-94
Bethel (Town) [1,681]	May.-C	5 Commissioners & Mayor	Elected-2	AL	2	Plurality	Pr. 1873-74, c. 20 SL 1953, c. 609
Beulaville (Town) [1,067]	C-Man.	5 Commissioners & Mayor	Elected-4	AL	4S	Plurality	SL 1975, c. 136 GS 160A-101
Biltmore Forest (Town) [1,440]	May.-C	3 Commissioners & Mayor	Elected-2	AL	2	Plurality	Pr. 1923, c. 32 GS 160A-66
Biscoe (Town) [1,700]	May.-C	5 Commissioners & Mayor	Elected-2	AL	4S	Plurality	Pr. 1901, c. 24 SL 1963, c. 656 GS 160A-66
Bladenboro (Town) [1,718]	May.-C	6 Commissioners & Mayor	Elected-4	DAL	4S	Plurality	SL 1974, c. 1270 GS 160A-101
Blowing Rock (Town) [1,418]	C-Man.	5 Commissioners & Mayor	Elected-2	AL	4S	Plurality	SL 1973, c. 419 GS 160A-101
Boonville (Town) [1,138]	May.-C	5 Commissioners & Mayor	Elected-4	AL	4S	Plurality	SL 1949, c 363 SL 1981(82), c. 1143
Broadway (Town) [1,015]	C-Man.	5 Commissioners & Mayor	Elected-4	AL	4S	Plurality	SL 1947, c. 548 SL 1997-416 SL 1999-230
Bryson City (Town) [1,411]	C-Man.	4 Aldermen & Mayor	Elected-4	AL	4S	Plurality	Pr. 1891, c. 207 SL 1955, c. 284 GS 160A-101

City (Style) [Population]	Form of Government	Governing Body	Mayor: Selection and Term	Board: Selection and Term		Election Method	Statutory Citations

1,000 to 2,500 (continued)

City (Style) [Population]	Form of Government	Governing Body	Mayor: Selection and Term	Board: Selection and Term		Election Method	Statutory Citations
Burnsville (Town) [1,623]	May.-C	4 Commissioners & Mayor	Elected-4	AL	4S	Plurality	Mun. Bd. Control 1922 GS 160A-66 GS 160A-101
Cape Carteret (Town) [1,214]	May.-C	5 Commissioners & Mayor	Elected-2	AL	4S	Plurality	SL 1959, c. 727 SL 1963, c. 929 SL 1969, c. 284 GS 160A-101
Carolina Shores (Town) [1,482]	May.-C	5 Commissioners & Mayor	Elected-4	AL	4S	Plurality	SL 1998-75
Carthage (Town) [1,871]	C-Man.	5 Council Members & Mayor	Elected-4	AL	4S	Plurality	SL 1999-239
Chadbourn (Town) [2,129]	C-Man.	5 Council Members & Mayor	Elected-2	AL	4S	Plurality	SL 1989(90), c. 895
Claremont (Town) [1,038]	C-Man.	5 Council Members & Mayor	Elected-2	AL	4S	Plurality	SL 1961, c. 76 SL 1975, c. 97 GS 160A-101
Clyde (Town) [1,324]	May.-C	4 Aldermen & Mayor	Elected-4	AL	4S	Plurality	Pr. 1889, c. 189 SL 1959, c. 1107 GS 160A-101
Coats (Town) [1,845]	May.-C	5 Commissioners & Mayor	Elected-2	AL	4S	Plurality	Pr. 1905, c. 362 SL 1969, c. 160 GS 160A-101
Connelly Springs (Town) [1,814]	May.-C	6 Aldermen & Mayor	Elected-4	AL	4S	Plurality	SL 1989, c. 528 SL 1993, c. 37
Creedmoor (City) [2,232]	C-Man.	5 Commissioners & Mayor	Elected-2	AL	4S	Plurality	SL 1969, c. 826 GS 160A-101
Denton (Town) [1,450]	May.-C	5 Commissioners & Mayor	Elected-2	AL	4S	Plurality	SL 1965, c. 497
Dobson (Town) [1,457]	May.-C	5 Commissioners & Mayor	Elected-4	AL	4S	Plurality	SL 1975, c. 232 GS 160A-101
Drexel (Town) [1,938]	C-Man.	4 Aldermen & Mayor	Elected-2	AL	4S	Plurality	Pr. 1913, c. 24 GS 160A-66, -101
East Spencer (Town) [1,755]	May.-C	6 Aldermen & Mayor	Elected-2	AL	4S	Plurality	SL 1973, c. 374

1,000 to 2,500 (continued)

City (Style) [Population]	Form of Government	Governing Body	Mayor: Selection and Term	Board: Selection and Term		Election Method	Statutory Citations
Ellerbe (Town) [1,021]	May.-C	5 Commissioners & Mayor	Elected-2	AL	4S	Plurality	Pr. 1931, c. 24 SL 1967, c. 310
Elm City (Town) [1,165]	May.-C	5 Commissioners & Mayor	Elected-2	AL	2	Plurality	SL 1955, c. 152
Enfield (Town) [2,347]	May.-C[1]	5 Commissioners & Mayor	Elected-4	4D 1AL	4S	Plurality	SL 1993, c. 479
Fair Bluff (Town) [1,181]	May.-C	5 Commissioners & Mayor	Elected-4	AL	4S	Plurality	Pr. Ex. 1913, c. 25 SL 1983(84), c. 1007
Four Oaks (Town) [1,424]	May.-C	5 Commissioners & Mayor	Elected-4	AL	4S	Plurality	SL 1953, c. 65 GS 160A-101
Franklinton (Town) [1,745]	May.-C	5 Commissioners & Mayor	Elected-4	AL	4S	Plurality	SL 1993, c. 160
Franklinville (Town) 1017 [1,258]	May.-C	5 Commissioners & Mayor	Elected-2	AL	4S	Plurality	SL 1983(84), c.
Fremont (Town) [1,463]	May.-C	6 Aldermen & Mayor	Elected-4	D	4	Plurality	Pr. 1913, c. 236 SL 1957, c. 66 SL 1971, c. 113 GS 160A-101
Garysburg (Town) [1,254]	May.-C	5 Commissioners & Mayor	Elected-2	AL	2	Plurality	SL 1985, c. 56
Glen Alpine (Town) [1,090]	May.-C	5 Aldermen & Mayor	Elected-4	AL	4S	Plurality	Pr. 1883, c. 61 SL 1989, c. 131
Granite Quarry (Town) [2,175]	May.-C	4 Aldermen	By & from Board[2]	AL	2	Plurality	Pr. 1901, c. 259 Pr. 1905, c. 43 SL 1957, c. 14
Greenlevel (Town) [2,042]	May.-C	5 Council Members	By & from Board[2]	AL	4S	Plurality	SL 1989(90), c. 942
Grifton (Town) [2,073]	May.-C	5 Commissioners & Mayor	Elected-4	AL	4S	Plurality	SL 1975, c. 480
Haw River (Town) [1,908]	C-Man.	4 Council Members & Mayor	Elected-2	AL	4S	Plurality	SL 1973, c. 234 SL 1974, c. 895 GS 160A-101
Hertford (Town) [2,070]	C-Man.	4 Commissioners & Mayor	Elected-4	AL	4S	Plurality	SL 1965, c. 586

City (Style) [Population]	Form of Government	Governing Body	Mayor: Selection and Term	Board: Selection and Term		Election Method	Statutory Citations

1,000 to 2,500 (continued)

City (Style) [Population]	Form of Government	Governing Body	Mayor: Selection and Term	Board: Selection and Term		Election Method	Statutory Citations
Hildebran (Town) [1,472]	May.-C	5 Commissioners & Mayor	Elected-4	AL	4S	Plurality	Pr. 1899, c. 212 SL 1973, c. 433 SL 1993, c. 238
Jefferson (Town) [1,422]	C-Man.	5 Aldermen & Mayor	Elected-4	AL	4S	Plurality	SL 1957, c. 552 GS 160A-101
Jonesville (Town) [2,259]	C-Man.	5 Council Members & Mayor	Elected-4	AL	4S	Plurality	SL 2001-16
Kenansville (Town) [1,149]	May.-C	5 Commissioners & Mayor	Elected-4	AL	4S	Plurality	SL 1967, c. 1194
Kenly (Town) [1,569]	C-Man.	5 Council Members & Mayor	Elected-2	AL	4S	Plurality	SL 1985, c. 14
Kure Beach (Town) [1,507]	May.-C	5 Commissioners	Elected-2	AL	4S	Plurality	SL 1947, c. 906 SL 1975, c. 484 GS 160A-101
Lake Lure (Town) [1,027]	C-Man.	4 Commissioners & Mayor	Elected-2	AL	4S	Plurality	SL 1987, c. 194
Lake Park (Village) [2,093]	May.-C	5 Council Members & Mayor	Elected-2	AL	4S	Plurality	SL 1993(94), c. 620
Lake Waccamaw (Town) [1,411]	C-Man.	4 Commissioners & Mayor	Elected-2	D	4S	Plurality	SL 1967, c. 14 GS 160A-101
Laurel Park (Town) [1,835]	C-Man.	4 Commissioners & Mayor	Elected-4	AL	4S	Plurality	SL 2000-8
Leland (Town) [1,931]	C-Man.	4 Council Members & Mayor	Elected-2	AL	4S	Plurality	SL 1989, c. 564 GS 160A-101
Locust (City) [2,416]	May.-C	7 Council Members & Mayor	Elected-2	AL	4S	Plurality	SL 1973, c. 246 SL 1977, c. 41
Madison (Town) [2,262]	C-Man.	6 Aldermen & Mayor	Elected-2	AL	2	Plurality	SL 1973, c. 289
Manteo (Town) [1,052]	C-Man.	6 Commissioners & Mayor	Elected-2	AL	4S	Plurality	Pr. 1899, c. 66 Pr. 1907, c. 198 SL 1993, c. 108 GS 160A-101
Mars Hill (Town) [1,764]	May.-C	3 Aldermen & Mayor	Elected-2	AL	2	Plurality	SL 1953, c. 890

City (Style) [Population]	Form of Government	Governing Body	Mayor: Selection and Term	Board: Selection and Term		Election Method	Statutory Citations

1,000 to 2,500 (continued)

City (Style) [Population]	Form of Government	Governing Body	Mayor: Selection and Term	Board: Selection and Term		Election Method	Statutory Citations
Marshville (Town) [2,360]	May.-C	5 Council Members & Mayor	Elected-2	AL	4S	Plurality	Pr. 1913, c. 313 SL 1973, c. 652 SL 2000-62
Marvin (Village) [1,039]	May.-C	4 Council Members & Mayor	Elected-2	AL	4S	Plurality	SL 1993 (94), c. 641
Mayodan (Town) [2,417]	C-Man.	5 Council Members & Mayor	Elected-2	AL	4S	Plurality	SL 1973, c. 501 GS 160A-101
Maysville (Town) [1,002]	May.-C	5 Commissioners & Mayor	Elected-2	AL	2	Plurality	Pr. 1897, c. 171 GS 163-279
Mineral Springs (Town) [1,370]	May.-C	6 Council Members & Mayor	Elected-2	AL	4S	Plurality	SL 1999-175
Mount Gilead (Town) [1,389]	May.-C	4 Commissioners & Mayor	Elected-2	AL	4S	Plurality	Pr. 1913, c. 133 SL 1957, c. 163
Mount Pleasant (Town) [1,259]	May.-C	5 Commissioners & Mayor	Elected-2	AL	2	Plurality	Pr. 1883, c. 77 Pr. 1931, c. 148
Murfreesboro (Town) [2,045]	May.-C	5 Council Members & Mayor	Elected-2	AL	2	Plurality	SL 1983, c. 445
Murphy (Town) [1,568]	May.-C	6 Commissioners & Mayor	Elected-4	AL	4	Partisan	SL 1979, c. 261
Norlina (Town) [1,107]	May.-C	5 Commissioners & Mayor	Elected-2	AL	2	Plurality	SL 1947, c. 1020 SL 1969, c. 95
Norwood (Town) [2,216]	May.-C	5 Commissioners & Mayor	Elected-4	AL	4S	Majority	Pr. 1905, c. 212 SL 2001-15
Oakboro (Town) [1,198]	May.-C	5 Commissioners & Mayor	Elected-2	AL	2	Plurality	Pr. 1915, c. 51
Pembroke (Town) [2,399]	C-Man.	4 Commissioners & Mayor	Elected-4	AL	4S	Plurality	Pr. 1895, c. 171 SL 1961, c. 97 SL 1974, c. 1289 GS 160A-66, -101 GS 163-279
Pilot Mountain (Town) [1,281]	C-Man.	4 Commissioners & Mayor	Elected-2	AL	4S	Plurality	SL 1971, c. 28 GS 160A-101
Pinebluff (Town) [1,109]	May.-C	5 Commissioners & Mayor	Elected-2	AL	2	Plurality	SL 1979, c. 243 GS 160A-101

City (Style) [Population]	Form of Government	Governing Body	Mayor: Selection and Term	Board: Selection and Term		Election Method	Statutory Citations

1,000 to 2,500 (continued)

City (Style) [Population]	Form of Government	Governing Body	Mayor: Selection and Term	Board: Selection and Term		Election Method	Statutory Citations
Pine Knoll Shores (Town) [1,524]	May.-C	6 Commissioners	By & from Board-2	AL	4S	Plurality	SL 1973, c. 265
Pine Level (Town) [1,313]	May.-C	4 Commissioners & Mayor	Elected-2	AL	2	Plurality	Pr. 1907, c. 425 SL 1957, c. 50
Pinetops (Town) [1,419]	May.-C	5 Commissioners & Mayor	Elected-4	AL	4S	Plurality	Pr. Ex. 1921, c. 64 GS 160A-101
Pittsboro (Town) [2,216]	C-Man.	5 Commissioners & Mayor	Elected-2	AL	4S	Plurality	SL 1973, c. 348
Polkton (Town) [1,195]	May.-C	5 Commissioners & Mayor	Elected-2	AL	2	Plurality	SL 1969, c. 936
Princeton (Town) [1,066]	May.-C	4 Commissioners & Mayor	Elected-2	AL	4S	Plurality	Pr. 1860-61, c. 161 SL 1955, c. 150
Ramseur (Town) [1,588]	May.-C	5 Commissioners & Mayor	Elected-4[3]	AL	4S	Primary	Pr. 1895, c. 308 SL 1957, c. 108 GS 163-290 GS 160A-101
Ranlo (Town) [2,198]	May.-C	5 Commissioners & Mayor	Elected-2	AL	2	Plurality	SL 1963, c. 776
Robbins (Town) [1,195]	May.-C	5 Commissioners & Mayor	Elected-4	AL	4S	Plurality	Pr. 1935, c. 63 SL 1979, c. 230
Robersonville (Town) [1,731]	May.-C	5 Commissioners & Mayor	Elected-2	AL	2	Plurality	Pr. 1905, c. 59 SL 1951, c. 48
Rockwell (Town) [1,971]	May.-C	5 Commissioners & Mayor	Elected-2	AL	2	Plurality	SL 1959, c. 17 GS 163-279
Roseboro (Town) [1,267]	May.-C	5 Commissioners & Mayor	Elected-4	AL	4S	Plurality	Pr. 1891, c. 279 SL 1995, c. 18
Rose Hill (Town) [1,330]	May.-C	5 Commissioners & Mayor	Elected-4	AL	4S	Plurality	Pr. 1901, c. 67 SL 1969, c. 330
Rowland (Town) [1,146]	May.-C	4 Commissioners & Mayor	Elected-2	AL	4S	Plurality	SL 1998-105 SL 2000-45
Rural Hall (Town) [2,464]	C-Man.	4 Council Members & Mayor	Elected-4	AL	4S	Plurality	SL 1973(74), c. 1100 GS 160A-101

City (Style) [Population]	Form of Government	Governing Body	Mayor: Selection and Term	Board: Selection and Term		Election Method	Statutory Citations

1,000 to 2,500 (continued)

City (Style) [Population]	Form of Government	Governing Body	Mayor: Selection and Term	Board: Selection and Term		Election Method	Statutory Citations
Rutherford College (Town) [1,293]	May.-C	6 Council Members & Mayor	Elected-4	AL	4S	Plurality	SL 1977, c. 452
Saint Pauls (Town) [2,137]	May.-C[1]	6 Commissioners & Mayor	Elected-4	4D 2AL	4S	Plurality	SL 1991(92), c. 874 SL 1993, c. 158
Scotland Neck (Town) [2,362]	May.-C	5 Commissioners & Mayor	Elected-2	AL	4S	Plurality	Pr. 1901, c. 342 PL 1941, c. 106 SL 1951, c. 667 SL 1957, c. 267 SL 1973, c. 382
Shallotte (Town) [1,381]	May.-C	5 Aldermen & Mayor	Elected-4	AL	4S	Plurality	SL 1965, c. 235 GS 160A-101
Sharpsburg (Town) [2,421]	May.-C	5 Commissioners & Mayor	Elected-2	AL	2	Majority	Pr. 1913, c. 452 SL 1957, c. 393 GS 163-290
Snow Hill (Town) [1,514]	May.-C	5 Commissioners & Mayor	Elected-4	AL	4S	Plurality	SL 1977, c. 58
Southern Shores (Town) [2,201]	May.-C	5 Council Members & Mayor	By & from Council-2	AL	4S	Plurality	SL 1979, c. 203
Southport (City) [2,351]	C-Man.	6 Aldermen & Mayor	Elected-2	DAL	4S	Plurality	Pr. 1909, c. 345 SL 1961, c.56 SL 1983, c. 659
Sparta (Town) [1,817]	May.-C	4 Council Members & Mayor	Elected-4	AL	4S	Plurality	Mun. Bd. Control 1924 GS 160A-101
Spring Hope (Town) [1,261]	May.-C	5 Commissioners & Mayor	Elected-4	AL	4S	Plurality	Pr. 1889, c. 55 Pr. 1923, c. 207 SL 1973, c. 40
Spruce Pine (Town) [2,030]	C-Man.	4 Council Members & Mayor	Elected-2	AL	4S	Plurality	Pr. 1913, c. 335 SL 1995(96), c. 663 GS 160A-101
Stanfield (Town) [1,113]	May.-C	5 Commissioners & Mayor	Elected-2	AL	2	Plurality	SL 1957, c. 485
Stoneville (Town) [1,002]	May.-C	5 Council Members & Mayor	Elected-4	AL	4S	Plurality	SL 1983, c. 287 SL 1998-107 GS 160A-101

1,000 to 2,500 (continued)

City (Style) [Population]	Form of Government	Governing Body	Mayor: Selection and Term	Board: Selection and Term		Election Method	Statutory Citations
Sunset Beach (Town) [1,824]	May.-C[1]	5 Council Members & Mayor	Elected-2	AL	4S	Plurality	SL 1963, c. 93 SL 1965, c. 362 GS 160A-101
Surf City (Town) [1,393]	C-Man.	5 Council Members & Mayor	Elected-2	AL	4S	Plurality	SL 1963, c. 829 GS 160A-101
Swansboro (Town) [1,426]	C-Man.	4 Commissioners & Mayor	Elected-2	AL	4S	Plurality	Pr. 1895, c. 207 SL 1955, c. 443 GS 160A-101
Sylva (Town) [2,435]	C-Man.[4]	5 Commissioners & Mayor	Elected-4	AL	4S	Plurality	Pr. 1899, c. 72 SL 1957, c. 27 SL 1961, c. 31 SL 2000-30
Taylorsville (Town) [1,799]	C-Man.	3 Commissioners & Mayor	Elected-2	AL	2	Plurality	Pr. 1887, c. 86 PL 1939, c. 312 GS 160A-66
Tobaccoville (Village) [2,209]	May.-C	4 Council Members & Mayor	Elected-2	AL	4S	Plurality	SL 1991, c. 232
Troutman (Town) [1,592]	May.-C	5 Aldermen & Mayor	Elected-4	AL	4S	Plurality	SL 1981, c. 144
Tryon (Town) [1,760]	C-Man.	3 Commissioners & Mayor	Elected-2	AL	2/4S[5]	Plurality	SL 1971, c. 441
Walnut Cove (Town) [1,465]	C-Man.	4 Commissioners & Mayor	Elected-2	AL	2	Plurality	SL 1991, c. 447
Weaverville (Town) [2,416]	C-Man.	5 Commissioners & Mayor	Elected-2	AL	2	Plurality	Pr. 1909, c. 335 GS 160A-101
Weldon (Town) [1,374]	May.-C	5 Commissioners & Mayor	Elected-4	AL	4S	Plurality	Pr. 1891, c. 83 SL 1965, c. 131 GS 160A-101
West Jefferson (Town) [1,081]	May.-C	5 Aldermen & Mayor	Elected-4	AL	4S	Plurality	SL 1967, c. 326
Whispering Pines (Village) [2,090]	May.-C	5 Council Members	By & from Council[6]-2	AL	2	Plurality	SL 1969, c. 72 SL 1963, c. 207 SL 1965, c. 564
Wilson's Mills (Town) [1,291]	May.-C	5 Council Members & Mayor	Elected-4	AL	4S	Plurality	SL 1996 (2d extra), c. 12

City (Style) [Population]	Form of Government	Governing Body	Mayor: Selection and Term	Board: Selection and Term		Election Method	Statutory Citations
1,000 to 2,500 (continued)							
Windsor (Town) [2,283]	May.-C	5 Commissioners & Mayor	Elected-4	AL	4S	Primary	GS 160A-101
Wingate (Town) [2,406]	May.-C[1]	5 Commissioners & Mayor	Elected-4	AL	4S	Plurality	Pr. 1901, c. 55 GS 160A-101
Yanceyville (Town) [2,091]	C-Man.	4 Council Members & Mayor	Elected-2	AL	4S	Plurality	SL 1985, c. 501 SL 2000-86

1. The board has appointed an administrator to supervise town departments.
2. Mayor serves at the pleasure of the board.
3. The 4-year term for the mayor of Ramseur begins in 2003.
4. Council–manager form established by ordinance.
5. Two board members elected every 2 years. The 1 elected with highest vote serves 4 years; the 1 elected with lowest vote serves 2 years.
6. Charter denominates mayor as "President."

City (Style) [Population]	Form of Government	Governing Body	Mayor: Selection and Term	Board: Selection and Term		Election Method	Statutory Citations
500 to 1,000							
Alliance (Town) [781]	May.-C	5 Commissioners	Elected[1]-2	AL	2	Plurality	SL 1965, c. 760
Ansonville (Town) [636]	May.-C	5 Council Members & Mayor	Elected-2	AL	2	Plurality	Mun. Bd. Control 1928 GS 163-290
Aulander (Town) [888]	May.-C	5 Commissioners & Mayor	Elected-2	AL	2	Plurality	Pr. 1933, c. 95 PL 1939, c. 288 SL 1967, c. 20 GS 163-290
Aurora (Town) [583]	May.-C	4 Commissioners & Mayor	Elected-4	AL	4S	Plurality	SL 1969, c. 256 GS 160A-101
Bailey (Town) [670]	May.-C	5 Commissioners & Mayor	Elected-4	AL	4S	Plurality	SL 1967, c. 184
Banner Elk (Town) [811]	C-Man.	5 Commissioners & Mayor	Elected-2	AL	4S	Plurality	Pr. 1925, c. 124 GS 160A-101
Bayboro (Town) [741]	May.-C	3 Commissioners & Mayor	Elected-2	AL	2	Plurality	Pr. 1903, c. 110
Belwood (Town) 1208 [962]	May.-C	4 Commissioners & Mayor	Elected-4	AL	4S	Plurality	SL 1977(78), c. SL 1981, c. 114
Black Creek (Town) [714]	May.-C	5 Commissioners & Mayor	Elected-2	AL	2	Plurality	Pr. 1870, c. 104 SL 1951, c. 485 GS 160A-101
Bogue (Town) [590]	May.-C	5 Council Members & Mayor	Elected-2	AL	4S	Plurality	SL 1995, c. 286
Calabash (Town) [711]	May.-C	4 Commissioners & Mayor	Elected-4	DAL	4S	Plurality	SL 1973, c. 391 SL 1989, c. 593 SL 1999-16
Candor (Town) [825]	May.-C	5 Commissioners & Mayor	Elected-4	AL	4S	Plurality	Pr. Ex. 1908, c. 48 SL 1971, c. 576
Catawba (Town) [698]	May.-C	4 Commissioners & Mayor	Elected-2	AL	4S	Plurality	SL 1965, c. 224
Cedar Point (Town) 1005 [929]	May.-C	4 Council Members & Mayor	Elected-2	AL	4S	Plurality	SL 1987(88), c.

City (Style) [Population]	Form of Government	Governing Body	Mayor: Selection and Term	Board: Selection and Term		Election Method	Statutory Citations

500 to 1,000 (continued)

City (Style) [Population]	Form of Government	Governing Body	Mayor: Selection and Term	Board: Selection and Term		Election Method	Statutory Citations
Chocowinity (Town) [733]	May.-C	4 Commissioners & Mayor	Elected-2	AL	2	Plurality	SL 1959, c. 343
Clarkton (Town) [705]	May.-C	3 Commissioners & Mayor	Elected-2	AL	2	Plurality	SL 1955, c. 440 SL 1985, c. 36
Cleveland (Town) [808]	May.-C	5 Commissioners & Mayor	Elected-2	AL	4S	Plurality	SL 1927, c. 160 SL 1979(80), c. 1171 SL 1981, c. 262
Columbia (Town) [819]	C-Man.	5 Aldermen & Mayor	Elected-2	AL	4S	Majority	PL 1941, c. 423 GS 160A-101 GS 163-290
Columbus (Town) [992]	May.-C	3 Council Members & Mayor	Elected-2	AL	4/2S[2]	Plurality	SL 1985, c. 46
Conway (Town) [734]	May.-C	5 Commissioners & Mayor	Elected-2	AL	2	Plurality	Pr. 1913, c. 161
Cooleemee (Town) [905]	May.-C	4 Commissioners & Mayor	Elected-4	AL	4S	Plurality	SL 1985, c. 424
Dobbins Heights (Town) [936]	May.-C	4 Council Members & Mayor	Elected-2	AL	4S	Majority	SL 1983, c. 658
Dortches (Town) [809]	May.-C	4 Commissioners & Mayor	Elected-4	AL	4	Majority	SL 1977, c. 358
East Arcadia (Town) [524]	May.-C	5 Council Members & Mayor	Elected-4	AL	4S	Plurality	SL 1973(74), c. 954
East Bend (Town) [659]	May.-C	5 Commissioners & Mayor	Elected-2	AL	4/2S[3]	Plurality	Pr. 1887, c. 144 SL 1955, c. 611 SL 1985, c. 104
Faison (Town) [744]	May.-C	5 Commissioners & Mayor	Elected-2	AL	4S	Plurality	SL 1973, c. 378
Faith (Town) [695]	May.-C	5 Aldermen	By & from Board-2	AL	2	Plurality	SL 1961, c. 159 SL 1979(80), c. 1111
Fallston (Town) [603]	May.-C	4 Commissioners & Mayor	Elected-2	AL	2	Plurality	SL 1971, c. 784
Fountain (Town) [533]	May.-C	5 Commissioners & Mayor	Elected-2	AL	4S	Plurality	Pr. 1923, c. 254 PL 1951, c. 724 GS 160A-101

City (Style) [Population]	Form of Government	Governing Body	Mayor: Selection and Term	Board: Selection and Term		Election Method	Statutory Citations
500 to 1,000 (continued)							
Garland (Town) [808]	May.-C	5 Commissioners & Mayor	Elected-2	AL	4S	Plurality	SL 1979, c. 393
Gaston (Town) [973]	May.-C	5 Commissioners & Mayor	Elected-2	AL	2	Plurality	SL 1949, c. 1153 GS 160A-66
Gibson (Town) [584]	May.-C	5 Commissioners & Mayor	Elected-2	AL	2	Plurality	Pr. 1899, c. 163
Greenevers (Town) [560]	May.-C	5 Council Members	Elected-2	AL	2	Plurality	Mun. Bd. Control
Grover (Town) [698]	May.-C	5 Commissioners & Mayor	Elected-4	AL	4S	Plurality	SL 1963, c. 812 GS 160A-101
Hamilton (Town) [516]	May.-C	5 Commissioners & Mayor	Elected-2	AL	2	Plurality	SL 1945, c. 302
Harmony (Town) [526]	May.-C	4 Aldermen & Mayor	Elected-2	AL	2	Plurality	Mun. Bd. Control
Hemby Bridge (Town) [897]	May.-C	5 Aldermen	By & from Board[4]	AL	4S	Majority	SL 1998-143
Highlands (Town) [909]	May.-C	5 Commissioners & Mayor	Elected-4	AL	4S	Plurality	SL 1991, c. 519 GS 160A-101
High Shoals (City) [729]	May.-C	6 Council Members & Mayor	Elected-2	AL	4S	Plurality	SL 1973, c. 317 GS 160A-101
Hoffman (Town) [624]	May.-C	5 Commissioners & Mayor	Elected-2	AL	2	Plurality	SL 1953, c. 1002
Holden Beach (Town) [787]	C-Man.	5 Commissioners & Mayor	Elected-2	AL	2	Plurality	Mun. Bd. Control GS 160A-101
Holly Ridge (Town) [831]	C-Man.	5 Council Members & Mayor	Elected-2	AL	2	Plurality	SL 1979, c. 87 GS 160A-101
Hot Springs (Town) [645]	May.-C	3 Aldermen & Mayor	Elected-2	AL	2	Plurality	Pr. 1929, c. 210 GS 163-279
Jackson (Town) [695]	May.-C	5 Commissioners & Mayor	Elected-4	AL	4S	Plurality	SL 1983, c. 286
Jamesville (Town) [502]	May.-C	5 Commissioners & Mayor	Elected-2	AL	4S	Plurality	SL 1951, c. 232 GS 160A-101

City (Style) [Population]	Form of Government	Governing Body	Mayor: Selection and Term	Board: Selection and Term		Election Method	Statutory Citations

500 to 1,000 (continued)

City (Style) [Population]	Form of Government	Governing Body	Mayor: Selection and Term	Board: Selection and Term		Election Method	Statutory Citations
Kingstown (Town) [845]	May.-C	5 Council Members & Mayor	Elected-4	AL	4S	Majority	SL 1989, c. 632
Lawndale (Town) [642]	May.-C	5 Commissioners & Mayor	Elected-4	AL	4S	Plurality	SL 1953, c. 492
Lewiston Woodville (Town) [613]	May.-C	5 Council Members & Mayor	Elected-2	4DAL 1AL	2	Plurality	SL 1981, c. 266
Littleton (Town) [692]	May.-C	5 Commissioners & Mayor	Elected-4	AL	4S	Plurality	SL 1963, c. 399 SL 1998-11
Lucama (Town) [847]	May.-C	5 Commissioners & Mayor	Elected-4	AL	4S	Plurality	SL 1977, c. 117
McAdenville (Town) [619]	May.-C	5 Council Members & Mayor	Elected-2	AL	2	Plurality	GS 160A-101 GS 163-279, -290
Maggie Valley (Town) [607]	C-Man.	4 Aldermen & Mayor	Elected-4	AL	4S	Plurality	SL 1973(74), c. 1337 SL 1995(96), c. 558 GS 160A-101
Magnolia (Town) [932]	May.-C	5 Commissioners & Mayor	Elected-4	AL	4S	Plurality	Pr. 1905, c. 174 SL 1963, c. 82
Marshall (Town) [840]	May.-C	3 Aldermen & Mayor	Elected-2	AL	2	Plurality	Pr. 1905, c. 165 Pr. 1913, c. 232 Pr. 1923, c. 35
Middlesex (Town) [838]	May.-C	5 Commissioners & Mayor	Elected-2	AL	4S	Plurality	Pr. 1908, c. 21 SL 1953, c. 1178 SL 1961, c. 44 GS 160A-101
Montreat (Town) [630]	May.-C	5 Commissioners & Mayor	Elected-4	AL	4S	Plurality	SL 1985, c. 295 SL 1998-38 GS 160A-101
Morven (Town) [579]	May.-C	5 Council Members & Mayor	Elected-2	AL	2	Plurality	SL 1947, c. 765 GS 160A-101
Newland (Town) [704]	May.-C	5 Aldermen & Mayor	Elected-2	AL	4S	Plurality	Pr. 1913, c. 275 SL 1951, c. 222 GS 160A-101
Newton Grove (Town) [606]	May.-C	5 Aldermen & Mayor	Elected-2	AL	4S	Plurality	Pr. 1935, c. 162 GS 160A-101

City (Style) [Population]	Form of Government	Governing Body	Mayor: Selection and Term	Board: Selection and Term		Election Method	Statutory Citations
500 to 1,000 (continued)							
North Topsail Beach (Town) [843]	C-Man.	5 Aldermen & Mayor	Elected-2	AL	4S	Plurality	SL 1989, c. 100
Northwest (City) [671]	May.-C	5 Council Members & Mayor	Elected-2	AL	4S	Plurality	SL 1993, c. 222
Old Fort (Town) [963]	May.-C	5 Aldermen & Mayor	Elected-4	AL	4	Plurality	Pr. 1911, c. 271
Oriental (Town) [875]	May.-C[5]	5 Commissioners & Mayor	Elected-2	AL	2	Plurality	Pr. 1899, c. 184 SL 1991(92), c. 878 SL 1993, c. 4 GS 163-279
Patterson Springs (Town) [620]	May.-C	5 Commissioners	By & from Board-4	AL	4	Plurality	SL 1974, c. 129
Peachland (Town) [554]	May.-C	5 Commissioners & Mayor	Elected-4	AL	4S	Plurality	SL 1947, c. 766 SL 1979, c. 340
Pikeville (Town) [719]	May.-C	5 Commissioners & Mayor	Elected-4	AL	4S	Plurality	Pr. 1891, c. 108 SL 1977, c. 20
Pink Hill (Town) [521]	May.-C	3 Commissioners & Mayor	Elected-2	AL	2	Plurality	Pr. 1915, c. 31 Pr. 1933, c. 221 SL 1955, c. 760
Polkville (Town) [535]	May.-C	4 Commissioners & Mayor	Elected-4	AL	4S	Plurality	SL 1971, c. 178 SL 1979, c. 266
Princeville (Town) [940]	C-Man.	4 Commissioners & Mayor	Elected-4	D	4	Plurality	SL 1977, c. 688 GS 160A-101
Richfield (Town) [515]	May.-C	5 Commissioners & Mayor	Elected-2	AL	2	Plurality	SL 1953, c. 1066 SL 1961, c. 527 GS 163-279
Richlands (Town) [928]	May.-C	5 Aldermen & Mayor	Elected-2	AL	2	Plurality	Pr. 1905, c. 47 SL 1949, c. 476
Rich Square (Town) [931]	May.-C	5 Commissioners & Mayor	Elected-2	AL	2	Primary	Pr. 1883, c. 128 GS 160A-66
Robbinsville (Town) [747]	May.-C	3 Aldermen & Mayor	Elected-4	AL	4	Plurality	Pr. 1923, c. 190 SL 1981, c. 194

City (Style) [Population]	Form of Government	Governing Body	Mayor: Selection and Term	Board: Selection and Term		Election Method	Statutory Citations

500 to 1,000 (continued)

City (Style) [Population]	Form of Government	Governing Body	Mayor: Selection and Term	Board: Selection and Term		Election Method	Statutory Citations
Rolesville (Town) [907]	May.-C	5 Commissioners & Mayor	Elected-2	AL	2	Plurality	PL 1941, c. 84
Roper (Town) [613]	May.-C	4 Commissioners & Mayor	Elected-2	AL	4S	Plurality	Pr. 1907, c. 24 GS 160A-101 GS 163-279
Saluda (City) [575]	May.-C	4 Commissioners & Mayor	Elected-4	AL	4S	Plurality	Pr. 1933, c. 123
Seaboard (Town) [695]	May.-C	5 Commissioners & Mayor	Elected-2	AL	2	Plurality	Pub. 1877, c. 208 GS 160A-101 GS 163-279, -290
Sedalia (Town) [618]	May.-C	5 Council Members	By & from Council[4]	AL	4S	Plurality	SL 1997-444
Stantonsburg (Town) 1212 [726]	C-Man.	5 Commissioners & Mayor	Elected-4	AL	4S	Plurality	SL 1977(78), c. GS 160A-101
Star (Town) [807]	May.-C	5 Commissioners & Mayor	Elected-2	AL	4S	Plurality	SL 1957, c. 448
Stedman (Town) [664]	May.-C	5 Commissioners & Mayor	Elected-2	AL	2	Plurality	Pr. 1913, c. 67 SL 1953, c. 409
St. James (Town) [804]	C-Man.	5 Council Members	By & from Council-2	AL	2	Plurality	SL 1999-241
Swepsonville (Town) [922]	May.-C	5 Council Members	By & from Council-4	AL	4S	Plurality	1997-448
Taylortown (Town) [845]	May.-C	5 Council Members	By & from Council[4]	AL	2	Plurality	SL 1987, c. 601
Vanceboro (Town) [898]	May.-C	5 Aldermen & Mayor	Elected-2	AL	2	Plurality	Pr. 1929, c. 26
Vass (Town) [750]	May.-C	5 Commissioners & Mayor	Elected-2	AL	2	Plurality	Pr. 1907, c. 807 SL 1953, c. 817 GS 160A-101
Wagram (Town) [801]	May.-C	5 Commissioners & Mayor	Elected-2	AL	4S	Plurality	Pr. 1911, c. 161 SL 1981, c. 404
Walnut Creek (Village) [859]	May.-C	5 Council Members	By & from Council[4]	AL	4S	Plurality	SL 1975, c. 687

City (Style) [Population]	Form of Government	Governing Body	Mayor: Selection and Term	Board: Selection and Term		Election Method	Statutory Citations

500 to 1,000 (continued)

City (Style) [Population]	Form of Government	Governing Body	Mayor: Selection and Term	Board: Selection and Term		Election Method	Statutory Citations
Warrenton (Town) [811]	May.-C[5]	7 Commissioners & Mayor	Elected-4	AL	4S	Plurality	Pr. 1915, c. 201 GS 160A-101
Whitakers (Town) [799]	May.-C	5 Commissioners & Mayor	Elected-4	AL	4S	Plurality	SL 1965, c. 996 SL 1979, c. 311
White Lake (Town) [529] 1160	May.-C	6 Commissioners & Mayor	Elected-4	AL	4S	Plurality	SL 1951, c. 511 SL 1967, c. 200 SL 1981(82), c. GS 160A-101
Whitsett (Town) [686]	May.-C	5 Council Members	By & from Council[4]	AL	4S	Plurality	SL 1991, c. 684
Winfall (Town) 773 [554]	May.-C	4 Commissioners & Mayor	Elected-2	AL	4S	Plurality	SL 1971, c. 342, GS 160A-101
Winton (Town) [956]	May.-C	5 Commissioners & Mayor	Elected-2	AL	2	Plurality	SL 1961, c. 674
Woodland (Town) [833]	May.-C	4 Commissioners & Mayor	Elected-2	AL	2	Plurality	Pr. 1883, c. 136 GS 163-279
Youngsville (Town) [651]	May.-C	5 Commissioners & Mayor	Elected-4	AL	4S	Plurality	GS 160A-101

1. Mayor is to be commissioner with largest vote in popular election.
2. Two board members elected every 2 years. The 1 elected with highest vote serves 4 years; the 1 elected with lowest vote serves 2 years.
3. Three board members elected every 2 years. The 2 elected with highest vote serve 4 years; the 1 elected with lowest vote serves 2 years.
4. Mayor serves at pleasure of council.
5. The board has appointed an administrator to supervise town departments.

City (Style) [Population]	Form of Government	Governing Body	Mayor: Selection and Term	Board: Selection and Term		Election Method	Statutory Citations
UNDER 500							
Alamance (Village) [310]	May.-C	6 Aldermen & Mayor	Elected-2	AL	4S	Plurality	SL 1979, c. 840
Arapahoe (Town) [436]	May.-C	5 Commissioners & Mayor	Elected-2	AL	2	Plurality	Mun. Bd. Control SL 1969, c. 200
Askewville (Town) [180]	May.-C	3 Commissioners & Mayor	Elected-2	AL	2	Plurality	PL 1951, c. 1153
Atkinson (Town) [236]	May.-C	4 Aldermen & Mayor	Elected-2	DAL	4S	Plurality	Pr. 1921, c. 163 GS 160A-101
Autryville (Town) [196]	May.-C[1]	5 Commissioners & Mayor	Elected-2	AL	4S	Plurality	PL 1991, c. 384
Bakersville (Town) [357]	May.-C[1]	3 Aldermen & Mayor	Elected-2	AL	2	Plurality	SL 1955, c. 1291
Bald Head Island (Village) [173]	C-Man.	5 Council Members	By & from Council-2	AL	4S	Plurality	SL 1997-324
Bath (Town) [275]	May.-C[1]	4 Commissioners & Mayor	Elected-2	AL	2	Plurality	PL 1941, c. 175 SL 1959, c. 189
Bear Grass (Town) [53]	May.-C	5 Commissioners & Mayor	Elected-2	AL	2	Plurality	PL 1909, c. 74 SL 1961, c. 1128
Beech Mountain (Town) [310]	C-Man.	5 Council Members	Council Member with most votes-2	AL	2	Plurality	SL 1981, c. 246
Belville (Town) [285]	May.-C	4 Commissioners & Mayor	Elected-2	AL	4S	Plurality	SL 1977, c. 84
Bethania (Town) [354]	May.-C	5 Commissioners	By & from Board[2]	AL	4S	Plurality	SL 1995, c. 74
Boardman (Town) [202]	May.-C	5 Council Members & Mayor	Elected-4	AL	4	Plurality	SL 1991(92), c. 876
Bolivia (Town) [148]	C-Man.	4 Aldermen & Mayor	Elected-2	AL	2	Plurality	PL 1961, c. 366
Bolton (Town) [494]	May.-C	5 Aldermen & Mayor	Elected-2	AL	4S	Plurality	SL 1977, c. 271

City (Style) [Population]	Form of Government	Governing Body	Mayor: Selection and Term	Board: Selection and Term		Election Method	Statutory Citations
Bostic (Town) [328]	May.-C	5 Commissioners & Mayor	Elected-2	AL	2	Plurality	Pr. 1913, c. 263
Bridgeton (Town) [328]	May.-C	4 Commissioners & Mayor	Elected-2	AL	2	Plurality	SL 1989, c. 621
Brookford (Town) [434]	May.-C	4 Aldermen & Mayor	Elected-2	AL	2	Plurality	SL 1961, c. 109 GS 163-279
Brunswick (Town) [360]	May.-C	5 Commissioners & Mayor	By & from Board-2	AL	2	Plurality	Pr. 1925, c. 197
Bunn (Town) [357]	May.-C	4 Commissioners & Mayor	Elected-2	AL	2	Plurality	SL 1963, c. 690
Calypso (Town) [410]	May.-C	5 Commissioners & Mayor	Elected-2	AL	2	Plurality	Pr. 1913, c. 264
Cameron (Town) [151]	May.-C	5 Commissioners & Mayor	Elected-4	AL	4S	Plurality	Laws 1876-77, c. 14 GS 163-279 GS 160A-101
Casar (Town) [308]	May.-C	3 Commissioners & Mayor	Elected-4	AL	4	Plurality	PL 1903, c. 359 SL 1971, c. 775 GS 160A-101
Castalia (Town) [340]	May.-C	5 Commissioners & Mayor	Elected-4	AL	4S	Plurality	SL 1987(88), c. 952
Caswell Beach (Town) [370]	May.-C	5 Commissioners & Mayor	Elected-4	AL	4S	Plurality	SL 1975, c. 293 GS 160A-101
Cedar Rock (Town) [315]	May.-C	5 Council Members & Mayor	Elected-4	AL	4S	Plurality	SL 1997-317
Centerville (Town) [99]	May.-C	3 Commissioners & Mayor	Elected-2	AL	2	Plurality	SL 1965, c. 695
Cerro Gordo (Town) [244]	May.-C	5 Commissioners & Mayor	Elected-2	AL	4S	Plurality	SL 1973, c. 1044
Chimney Rock (Village) [175]	May.-C	5 Council Members	By & from Council[2]	AL	4S	Plurality	SL 1991, c. 444
Cofield (Village) [347]	May.-C	5 Council Members & Mayor	Elected-2	AL	2	Plurality	SL 1969, c. 587

City (Style) [Population]	Form of Government	Governing Body	Mayor: Selection and Term	Board: Selection and Term		Election Method	Statutory Citations
UNDER 500 (continued)							
Colerain (Town) [221]	May.-C	5 Commissioners & Mayor	Elected-2	AL	2	Primary	SL 1953, c. 290
Como (Town) [78]	May.-C	4 Commissioners & Mayor	Elected-2	AL	2	Plurality	SL 1967, c. 920
Conetoe (Town) [365]	May.-C	4 Commissioners & Mayor	Elected-2	AL	2	Plurality	Pr. 1887, c. 154 SL 1957, c. 278 SL 1959, c. 63
Cove City (Town) [433]	May.-C	5 Commissioners & Mayor	Elected-2	AL	2	Plurality	SL 1957, c. 427 GS 163-279
Creswell (Town) [278]	May.-C	4 Commissioners & Mayor	Elected-4	AL	2	Plurality	Pr. 1907, c. 276 SL 1993(94), c. 626 GS 163-279
Crossnore (Town) [242]	May.-C	5 Aldermen & Mayor	Elected-2	AL	4S/2[3]	Plurality	SL 1967, c. 832
Danbury (Town) [108]	May.-C	4 Council Members & Mayor	Elected-2	AL	4S	Plurality	SL 1991, c. 169 GS 160A-101
Dillsboro (Town) [205]	May.-C	5 Aldermen & Mayor	Elected-4	AL	4	Plurality	Pr. 1889, c. 177 Pr. 1907, c. 274 GS 163-279 GS 160A-101
Dover (Town) [443]	May.-C	5 Aldermen & Mayor	Elected-2	AL	2	Plurality	Pr. 1901, c. 275 GS 163-290
Dublin (Town) [250]	May.-C	3 Commissioners & Mayor	Elected-2	AL	2	Plurality	PL 1951, c. 509
Earl Station (Town) [234]	May.-C	4 Commissioners & Mayor	Elected-2	AL	2	Plurality	SL 1971, c. 787
East Laurinburg (Town) [295]	May.-C	3 Commissioners & Mayor	Elected-2	AL	2	Plurality	Pr. 1909, c. 221
Elk Park (Town) [459]	May.-C	5 Commissioners & Mayor	Elected-2	AL	2	Plurality	Pr. 1889, c. 256
Ellenboro (Town) [479]	May.-C	5 Council Members & Mayor	Elected-2	AL	2	Plurality	SL 1983, c. 425
Eureka (Town) [244]	May.-C	5 Commissioners & Mayor	Elected-4	AL	4S	Plurality	SL 1949, c. 459 SL 1981, c. 70

City (Style) [Population]	Form of Government	Governing Body	Mayor: Selection and Term	Board: Selection and Term		Election Method	Statutory Citations

UNDER 500 (continued)

City (Style) [Population]	Form of Government	Governing Body	Mayor: Selection and Term	Board: Selection and Term		Election Method	Statutory Citations
Everetts (Town) [179]	May.-C	3 Commissioners & Mayor	Elected-2	AL	2	Plurality	Pr. 1893, c. 321 SL 1979, c. 82
Falcon (Town) [328]	May.-C	4 Commissioners & Mayor	Elected-2	AL	2	Plurality	Pr. 1913, c. 318
Falkland (Town) [112]	May.-C	3 Commissioners & Mayor	Elected-2	AL	2	Plurality	PL 1947, c. 1059 SL 1985(86), c. 832
Forest Hills (Village) [330]	May.-C	4 Council Members & Mayor	Elected-2	AL	4S	Plurality	SL 1997-345
Foxfire Village (Village) [474]	May.-C	5 Council Members	By & from Council[2]	AL	4S	Plurality	SL 1977, c. 237
Gatesville (Town) [281]	May.-C	3 Commissioners & Mayor	Elected-2	AL	2	Plurality	Pr. 1923, c. 88
Godwin (Town) [112]	May.-C	3 Commissioners & Mayor	Elected-2	AL	2	Plurality	Pr. 1905, c. 397 SL 1947, c. 243 GS 163-279
Goldston (Town) [319]	May.-C	5 Commissioners & Mayor	Elected-2	AL	2	Plurality	Pr. 1907, c. 108 SL 1957, c. 704 GS 160A-101
Grandfather Village (Village) [73]	May.-C	4 Council Members & Mayor	Elected-2	AL	4S	Plurality	SL 1987, c. 419
Grantsboro (Town) [454]	May.-C	5 Council Members & Mayor	Elected-2	AL	2	Plurality	SL 1997-446
Grimesland (Town) [440]	May.-C	5 Aldermen	By & from Board-2	AL	2	Plurality	Pr. 1893, c. 222 SL 1957, c. 1153
Halifax (Town) [344]	May.-C	5 Commissioners & Mayor	Elected-2	AL	2	Plurality	[Unknown]
Harrells (Town) [187]	May.-C	5 Commissioners	By & from Board-2	AL	2	Plurality	SL 1969, c. 466
Harrellsville (Town) [102]	May.-C	5 Commissioners & Mayor	Elected-2	AL	2	Plurality	PL 1955, c. 92 PL 1983, c. 138
Hassell (Town) [72]	May.-C	5 Commissioners & Mayor	Elected-2	AL	2	Plurality	Pr. 1903, c. 96 SL 1965, c. 279

City (Style) [Population]	Form of Government	Governing Body	Mayor: Selection and Term	Board: Selection and Term		Election Method	Statutory Citations

UNDER 500 (continued)

City (Style) [Population]	Form of Government	Governing Body	Mayor: Selection and Term	Board: Selection	and Term	Election Method	Statutory Citations
Hayesville (Town) [297]	May.-C	3 Commissioners & Mayor	Elected-4	AL	4	Plurality	PL 1913, c. 468 SL 1977, c. 210
Hobgood (Town) [404]	May.-C	5 Commissioners & Mayor	Elected-2	AL	4S	Plurality	Pr. 1891, c. 160 Pr. 1903, c. 137 GS 160A-101
Hookerton (Town) 1020 [467]	May.-C	4 Commissioners & Mayor	Elected-2	AL	4S	Plurality	SL 1973(74), c.
Indian Beach (Town) [95]	May.-C	5 Commissioners	By & from Board-2	AL	4S	Plurality	SL 1973, c. 513
Kelford (Town) [245]	May.-C	5 Commissioners & Mayor	Elected-2	AL	2	Plurality	Pr. 1907, c. 163 GS 160A-101
Kittrell (Town) [148]	May.-C	3 Commissioners & Mayor	Elected-2	AL	2	Plurality	PL 1885, c. 136 GS 163-279
Lansing (Town) [151]	May.-C	5 Aldermen & Mayor	Elected-2	AL	2	Plurality	Mun. Bd. Control
Lasker (Town) [103]	May.-C	3 Commissioners & Mayor	Elected-2	AL	2	Plurality	Pr. 1895, c. 281 PL 1939, c. 48
Lattimore (Town) [419]	May.-C	3 Aldermen & Mayor	Elected-2	AL	2	Plurality	PL 1899, c. 52
Leggett (Town) [77]	May.-C	3 Commissioners & Mayor	Elected-4	AL	4	Plurality	SL 1973, c. 4 SL 1998-32 GS 160A-101
Lilesville (Town) [459]	May.-C	5 Commissioners & Mayor	Elected-2	AL	2	Plurality	SL 1947, c. 764
Linden (Town) [127]	May.-C	5 Commissioners & Mayor	Elected-2	AL	2	Plurality	Pr. 1913, c. 398 SL 2001-472
Love Valley (Town) [30]	May.-C	5 Commissioners & Mayor	Elected-2	AL	2	Plurality	Mun. Bd. Control
Lumber Bridge (Town) [118]	May.-C	4 Commissioners & Mayor	Elected-4	AL	4S	Plurality	Pr. 1911, c. 99 SL 1967, c. 226 SL 1995(96), c. 570
McDonald (Town) [119]	May.-C	3 Council Members & Mayor	Elected-2	AL	2	Plurality	Pr. 1911, c. 443 GS 163-279

City (Style) [Population]	Form of Government	Governing Body	Mayor: Selection and Term	Board: Selection and Term		Election Method	Statutory Citations

UNDER 500 (continued)

City (Style) [Population]	Form of Government	Governing Body	Mayor: Selection and Term	Board: Selection and Term		Election Method	Statutory Citations
McFarlan (Town) [89]	May.-C	5 Commissioners & Mayor	Elected-2	AL	2	Plurality	Pr. 1885, c. 102 PL 1947, c. 771
Macclesfield (Town) [458]	May.-C	4 Commissioners & Mayor	Elected-2	AL	4S	Plurality	SL 1949, c. 1124 GS 160A-101
Macon (Town) [115]	May.-C	5 Commissioners & Mayor	Elected-2	AL	2	Plurality	PL 1905, c. 246
Marietta (Town) [164]	May.-C	4 Council Members & Mayor	Elected-2	AL	4S	Plurality	SL 1985, c. 111
Mesic (Town) [257]	May.-C	5 Council Members & Mayor	Elected-2	AL	2	Plurality	SL 1971, c. 626 GS 160A-101
Micro (Town) [454]	May.-C	3 Commissioners & Mayor	Elected-2	AL	2	Plurality	SL 1963, c. 762
Middleburg (Town) [162]	May.-C	3 Council Members & Mayor	Elected-2	AL	2	Plurality	[Unknown]
Milton (Town) [132]	May.-C	4 Commissioners & Mayor	Elected-4	AL	4	Plurality	Pr. 1913, c. 130 PL 1967, c. 207
Minnesott Beach (Town) [311]	C-Man.	4 Commissioners & Mayor	Elected-2	AL	2	Plurality	SL 1971, c. 890
Momeyer (Town) [291]	May.-C	4 Council Members & Mayor	Elected-4	AL	4S	Plurality	SL 1991, c. 242 SL 1995, c. 212
Mooresboro (Town) 1209 [314]	May.-C	5 Commissioners & Mayor	Elected-4	AL	4S	Plurality	SL 1977(78), c. SL 1981, c. 113
Navassa (Town) [479]	May.-C	5 Council Members & Mayor	Elected-4	DAL	4S	Plurality	SL 1977, c. 77 SL 2001-325
New London (Town) [326]	May.-C	5 Commissioners & Mayor	Elected-4	AL	4S	Plurality	Pr. 1907, c. 91 SL 2001-131
Norman (Town) [72]	May.-C	3 Commissioners & Mayor	Elected-4	AL	4	Plurality	Pr. Ex. 1913, c. 74 GS 160A-101
Oak City (Town) [339]	May.-C	5 Commissioners & Mayor	Elected-2	AL	2	Primary	Pr. 1891, c. 100 Pr. 1905, c. 155 PL 1953, c. 66

City (Style) [Population]	Form of Government	Governing Body	Mayor: Selection and Term	Board: Selection and Term		Election Method	Statutory Citations
UNDER 500 (continued)							
Ocean Isle Beach (Town) [426]	May.-C	5 Commissioners & Mayor	Elected-2	AL	4S	Plurality	SL 1959, c. 887 SL 1965, c. 756 GS 160A-101
Orrum (Town) [79]	May.-C	4 Council Members & Mayor	Elected-2	AL	2	Plurality	SL 1983(84), c. 993
Pantego (Town) [170]	May.-C	5 Commissioners & Mayor	Elected-2	AL	2	Plurality	Pr. 1881, c. 93
Parkton (Town) [428]	May.-C	5 Commissioners & Mayor	Elected-2	AL	2	Plurality	SL 1945, c. 803
Parmele (Town) [290]	May.-C	3 Commissioners & Mayor	Elected-4	AL	4	Plurality	Pr. 1893, c. 60 GS 163-290 GS 160A-101
Peletier (Town) [487]	May.-C	5 Council Members & Mayor	Elected-2	AL	4S	Plurality	SL 1996 (2d Ex. Sess.), c. 1
Pollocksville (Town) [269]	May.-C	5 Commissioners & Mayor	Elected-4	AL	4S	Plurality	Pr. 1911, c. 163 SL 1965, c. 202 GS 160A-101 GS 163-279
Powellsville (Town) [259]	May.-C	3 Commissioners & Mayor	Elected-2	AL	2	Plurality	Pr. 1919, c. 94 GS 163-279
Proctorville (Town) [133]	May.-C	3 Council Members & Mayor	Elected-2	AL	2	Plurality	PL 1913, c. 369 SL 1963, c. 306 GS 160A-101
Raynham (Town) [67]	May.-C	3 Council Members & Mayor	Elected-2	AL	4S	Plurality	SL 1975, c. 388 SL 1977, c. 16 GS 160A-101
Rennert (Town) [283]	May.-C	5 Commissioners & Mayor	Elected-4	AL	4S	Plurality	SL 1977, c. 300 SL 2001-3
Rhodhiss (Town) [366]	May.-C	4 Commissioners & Mayor	Elected-4	AL	4S	Plurality	SL 1961, c. 471 SL 1985, c. 94
Ronda (Town) [460]	May.-C	5 Commissioners & Mayor	Elected-4	AL	4S	Plurality	Mun. Bd. Control GS 160A-101

City (Style) [Population]	Form of Government	Governing Body	Mayor: Selection and Term	Board: Selection and Term		Election Method	Statutory Citations

UNDER 500 (continued)

City (Style) [Population]	Form of Government	Governing Body	Mayor: Selection and Term	Board: Selection	and Term	Election Method	Statutory Citations
Rosman (Town) [490]	May.-C	5 Aldermen & Mayor	Elected-4	AL	4S	Plurality	Pr. 1901, c. 172 Pr. 1905, c. 105 GS 160A-101 GS 163-279
Roxobel (Town) [263]	May.-C	4 Commissioners & Mayor	Elected-2	AL	2	Plurality	Pr. 1911, c. 439
Ruth (Town) [329]	May.-C	2 Commissioners & Mayor	Elected-2	AL	2	Plurality	PL 1939, c. 53
Saint Helena (Village) [395]	May.-C	4 Council Members & Mayor	Elected-2	AL	4S	Plurality	SL 1987(88), c. 942
Salemburg (Town) [469]	May.-C	6 Commissioners & Mayor	Elected-4	AL	4S	Plurality	SL 1967, c. 104 SL 1993(94), c. 703
Sandy Creek (Town) [246]	May.-C	5 Council Members	By & from Council[2]	AL	4S	Plurality	SL 1987(88), c. 1007
Sandyfield (Town) [340]	May.-C	5 Council Members & Mayor	Elected-2	AL	4S	Plurality	SL 1993(94), c. 729
Santeetlah (Town) [67]	May.-C	5 Council Members	Council Member with most votes-2	AL	2	Plurality	SL 1987(88), c. 1012
Saratoga (Town) [379]	May.-C	3 Commissioners & Mayor	Elected-2	AL	2	Majority	SL 1947, c. 462
Seagrove (Town) [246]	May.-C	5 Commissioners & Mayor	Elected-2	AL	2	Plurality	Pr. 1913, c. 270
Seven Devils (Town) [129]	C-Man.	5 Council Members	By & from Board[2]	AL	4S/2[3]	Plurality	SL 1979, c. 205 GS 160A-101
Seven Springs (Town) [86]	May.-C	5 Commissioners & Mayor	Elected-2	AL	4S	Plurality	SL 1971, c. 21
Severn (Town) [263]	May.-C	5 Commissioners & Mayor	Elected-2	AL	2	Plurality	Pr. 1919, c. 39 SL 1953, c. 1176
Simpson (Village) [464]	May.-C	3 Council Members	Council Member with most votes-2	AL	2	Plurality	Mun. Bd. Control
Sims (Town) [128]	May.-C	5 Commissioners & Mayor	Elected-2	AL	2	Plurality	Pr. 1923, c. 58 SL 1953, c. 292

City (Style) [Population]	Form of Government	Governing Body	Mayor: Selection and Term	Board: Selection and Term		Election Method	Statutory Citations

UNDER 500 (continued)

City (Style) [Population]	Form of Government	Governing Body	Mayor: Selection and Term	Board: Selection and Term		Election Method	Statutory Citations
Speed (Town) [70]	May.-C	5 Commissioners & Mayor	Elected-2	AL	2	Plurality	Pr. 1923, c. 169 SL 1957, c. 279
Spencer Mountain (Town) [51]	May.-C	3 Commissioners & Mayor	Elected-2	AL	2	Plurality	SL 1963, c. 473
Staley (Town) [347]	May.-C	5 Commissioners & Mayor	Elected-2	AL	2	Plurality	Pr. 1901, c. 386 GS 163-279
Stem (Town) [229]	May.-C	5 Commissioners & Mayor	Elected-2	AL	2	Plurality	Pr. 1911, c. 183
Stonewall (Town) [285]	May.-C	3 Commissioners & Mayor	Elected-2	AL	2	Plurality	SL 1969, c. 385
Stovall (Town) [376]	May.-C	5 Commissioners & Mayor	Elected-4	AL	4S	Plurality	SL 1979, c. 596 SL 2001-100
Sugar Mountain (Village) [226]	C-Man.	4 Council Members & Mayor	Elected-2	AL	4S	Plurality	SL 1985, c. 395
Tar Heel (Town) [70]	May.-C	3 Council Members & Mayor	Elected-2	AL	2	Plurality	SL 1963, c. 763
Teachey (Town) [245]	May.-C	5 Commissioners & Mayor	Elected-2	AL	2	Plurality	SL 1957, c. 253
Topsail Beach (Town) [471]	C-Man.	5 Commissioners & Mayor	Elected-2	AL	2	Plurality	SL 1963, c. 67, 248 SL 1989, c. 153
Trenton (Town) [206]	May.-C	3 Commissioners & Mayor	Elected-2	AL	2	Plurality	Pr. 1911, c. 174 SL 1949, c. 879
Turkey (Town) [262]	May.-C	4 Commissioners & Mayor	Elected-2	AL	2	Plurality	Pr. 1913, c. 82
Vandemere (Town) [289]	May.-C	5 Commissioners & Mayor	Elected-2	AL	2	Plurality	Pr. 1895, c. 311 GS 163-279
Varnamtown (Town) 1003 [481]	May.-C	5 Aldermen & Mayor	Elected-2	AL	4S	Plurality	SL 1987(88), c.
Waco (Town) [328]	May.-C	3 Aldermen & Mayor	Elected-4	AL	4S	Plurality	Pr. 1907, c. 147 GS 160A-101

City (Style) [Population]	Form of Government	Governing Body	Mayor: Selection and Term	Board: Selection and Term		Election Method	Statutory Citations
UNDER 500 (continued)							
Wade (Town) [480]	May.-C	5 Commissioners & Mayor	Elected-2	AL	2	Plurality	PL 1913, c. 408 SL 1969, c. 89
Walstonburg (Town) [224]	May.-C	5 Commissioners & Mayor	Elected-2	AL	2	Plurality	Pr. 1913, c. 45
Washington Park (Town) [440]	May.-C	5 Commissioners & Mayor	Elected-2	AL	2	Plurality	Mun. Bd. Control SL 1949, c. 48
Watha (Town) [151]	May.-C	3 Commissioners & Mayor	Elected-2	AL	2	Plurality	Pr. 1909, c. 158 SL 1989(90), c. 884
Webster (Town) [486]	May.-C	5 Aldermen & Mayor	Elected-4	AL	4	Plurality	SL 1955, c. 423 SL 1957, c. 60 SL 1977, c. 171

1. The board has appointed an administrator to supervise town departments.
2. Mayor serves at pleasure of council.
3. Three candidates are elected every 2 years. The 2 elected with highest votes serve 4 years; the 1 elected with lowest vote serves 2 years.

SUMMARY

	23 cities over 25,000	39 cities 10,000– 25,000	44 cities 5,000– 10,000	83 cities 2,500– 5,000	118 cities 1,000– 2,500	96 cities 500– 1,000	138 cities under 500	541 cities TOTAL
STYLE OF CORPORATION								
City	21	19	18	6	3	3	0	70
Town	2	19	25	75	111	92	128	452
Village	0	1	1	2	4	1	10	19
STYLE OF GOVERNING BOARD								
Board of Commissioners	0	9	13	38	72	62	92	286
Board of Aldermen	2	5	4	14	17	14	16	72
Council	21	25	27	31	29	20	30	183
FORM OF GOVERNMENT								
Council–Manager	23	37	39	53	38	9	7	206
Mayor–Council	0	2	5	30	80	87	131	335
SELECTION OF MAYOR								
Mayor elected by the people	22	38	43	77	112	86	125	503
Mayor selected by & from governing board	1	1	1	6	6	9	10	34
Other	0	0	0	0	0	1	3	4

	23 cities over 25,000	39 cities 10,000–25,000	44 cities 5,000–10,000	83 cities 2,500–5,000	118 cities 1,000–2,500	96 cities 500–1,000	138 cities under 500	541 cities TOTAL
MAYOR'S TERM								
2-year terms	15	21	27	39	66	59	106	333
4-year terms	8	18	17	39	50	32	28	192
At board's pleasure	0	0	0	5	2	5	4	16
NUMBER OF MEMBERS OF GOVERNING BOARD								
11 members	1	0	0	0	0	0	0	1
9 members	1	0	0	0	0	0	0	1
8 members	4	6	2	0	0	0	0	12
7 members	4	7	3	1	1	1	0	17
6 members	11	7	7	15	12	2	2	56
5 members	1	14	24	48	75	68	76	306
4 members	1	5	8	18	26	18	28	104
3 members	0	0	0	1	4	7	31	43
2 members	0	0	0	0	0	0	1	1
TERM OF OFFICE OF GOVERNING BOARD								
2-year terms	10	9	9	16	24	37	82	187
4-year terms	3	1	4	2	3	5	9	27
Staggered 4-year terms	10	26	30	63	90	52	45	316
Other	0	3	1	2	1	2	2	11

	23 cities over 25,000	39 cities 10,000–25,000	44 cities 5,000–10,000	83 cities 2,500–5,000	118 cities 1,000–2,500	96 cities 500–1,000	138 cities under 500	541 cities TOTAL
MODE OF ELECTION OF GOVERNING BOARD								
Elected at large	7	21	30	70	109	93	136	466
Elected at large, but with district residence requirement	2	3	6	7	3	1	2	24
Combination of at-large members & members elected at large but repre-senting districts	2	0	2	1	1	1	0	7
Elected by & from districts	5	5	2	2	3	1	0	18
Combination of at-large & district members	7	10	4	3	2	0	0	26
TYPE OF ELECTION								
Partisan elections	2	2	1	3	1	0	0	9
Nonpartisan primary	8	5	2	5	3	1	0	24
Election determined by majority of votes cast, with runoff	5	7	5	3	2	5	1	28
Election decided by plurality	8	25	36	72	112	90	137	480

For Reference

Not to be taken from this room